WOMEN PREACHERS FORBIDDEN
OR NOT?

SHIRLEY HOLMES-SULTON

Order this book online at www.trafford.com
or email orders@trafford.com

Most Trafford titles are also available at major online book retailers.

Front Cover design by Master Tyrone Holmes Sr./tyronetv@bluebox.com

Print information available on the last page.

ISBN: 978-1-4907-6662-1 (sc)
ISBN: 978-1-4907-6664-5 (hc)
ISBN: 978-1-4907-6663-8 (e)

Library of Congress Control Number: 2015917984

Scripture quotations marked KJV are from the Holy Bible, King James Version
(Authorized Version). First published in 1611. Quoted from the KJV Classic
Reference Bible, Copyright © 1983 by The Zondervan Corporation

Trafford rev. 04/27/2017

 www.trafford.com

North America & international
toll-free: 1 888 232 4444 (USA & Canada)
fax: 812 355 4082

Contents

I will pour out my spirit upon all flesh, your sons and daughters shall prophesy. Joel 2:28

I will pour out my spirit upon all flesh, your sons and daughters shall prophesy. Joel 2:28

I will pour out my spirit upon all flesh, your sons and daughters shall prophesy. Joel 2:28

I will pour out my spirit upon all flesh, your sons and daughters shall prophesy. Joel 2:28

I will pour out my spirit upon all flesh, your sons and daughters shall prophesy. Joel 2:28

I will pour out my spirit upon all flesh, your sons and daughters shall prophesy. Joel 2:28

Preface

This book will focus on a few of the women in the Bible, there are over one hundred and twenty. I will expound on the most prominent ones, to help eradicate the myth that women shouldn't pastor or serve in any position usurping authority over men. Whereas we will find in the Old and New Testament they did. However, the men are the dominant ones, meaning their use by God is mentioned more than woman. One way Webster dictionary put it is like this, "Exercising the most influence or control governing." Now I don't have any problems with men being the head, because they are ordained by God to be the head, and I love it. But that doesn't mean a woman can't be in leadership with authority over men. It seem to me that being the head or in leadership from the male prospective, mean to give orders. And most have difficulty with taking orders from a woman in the religious sector. Leadership isn't about giving orders, but about working in harmony to accomplish

I will pour out my spirit upon all flesh, your sons and daughters shall prophesy. Joel 2:28

common goals. Our common goal should be to please our God.

Now men please, be the head, and lead the family spiritually, in a daily devotion with God, if it's only ten (10) minutes daily in His presence. Have teaching moments and sessions with the children, teaching them at an early age, the ways of God, as in Deuteronomy 6th chapter specifies. Stop leaving it up to the mother to do alone. Be a great example of love towards the weaker vessel and have a forgiving spirit towards all, especially the immediate family and the house hold of faith. Furthermore, no one is hindering men from being in leadership. My thing is, I don't think we have time to debate the issue while so many souls are being lost and dying while we're disputing over who should serve in religious leadership, the man, or woman. What seems to be said, is that God can only use men and not women. S U R P R I S E! He uses both.

The harvest is plenteous, but the laborers are few. We all need to be working towards a harvest. Paul declares in the New Testament, "There is neither Jew nor Greek, there is neither bond nor free, there is neither male nor female: for ye all are one in Christ Jesus" (**Galatians 3:28**). AMEN. Brothers and sisters let us get busy for the cause of Christ. There are so many dying souls, and hurting hearts.

I will pour out my spirit upon all flesh, your sons and daughters shall prophesy. Joel 2:28

Remember **Joel 2:28** said it like this in the Old Testament, "I will pour out my spirit on all flesh; and your sons and daughters shall prophesy", again we find in the New Testament **Acts 2:17,** stating, "And it shall come to pass in the last days, said God, I will pour out my Spirit upon all flesh: and your sons and your daughters shall prophesy". We all seem to agree that these are truly the last days, but have difficulty with the daughters prophesying. Did you know that the root word of prophesying is prophet? What does a prophet do? Preach the unadulterated Word of God. Now let all of us cut the nonsense out that's not profitable, and get busy for God. We are using God's valuable time and breadth for naught. Battling whether or not a woman should be classified as a preacher. What does a prophet do according to the Word of God? **II Peter 1:19-21,** let us know that true prophets/prophetess speak the word of God and not of man. We need to get busy and spend energy reaching the lost instead of having problems with female leaders, Pastors, and overseers, in the ministry. To be honest with you I had a problem with it myself in the beginning, until I begin to properly study God's Word. I found that Woman was included as well as men **(Galatians 4:22).** "But when the fullness of the time was come, God sent forth His Son, made of a woman" **(Galatians 4:4).** Know that God could have

I will pour out my spirit upon all flesh, your sons and daughters shall prophesy. Joel 2:28

sent His Son into this world by any means He so desired. Paul also commanded his fellow laborers to go, and help those women and Clement which worked with him in the gospel, as well as other fellow laborers that worked with him.

(Philippians 4:3). One of my mother's greatest sayings were, "if God can use a rooster and jackass, He can use a woman". Wow, what a revelation!

According to Mr. Webster's Dictionary, a prophet is: 1. "The chief spokesperson of a movement. 2. A man/woman who speaks by divine inspiration, or as the interpreter through whom the will of a god is expressed". Although Webster's Dictionary speaks of a god, we know it is not a god, but the God almighty, the true and living God.

The Bible in **I Peter 3:1**, speaks of wives leading their husbands to Christ. The wife might be the only example the husband may have of our Lord and Savior. Should she wait for a man to come along? Peter also said in that same **Chapter, verse 7**, for men to give honor to their wives according to their **knowledge,** and to work together as a team, so his prayers wouldn't be hindered. Some women are highly educated in both secular and the religious world. Some organizations ordain their women as missionaries and evangelist. Don't they know Paul was the first missionary and a man? So why a woman can only be a missionary or

I will pour out my spirit upon all flesh, your sons and daughters shall prophesy. Joel 2:28

evangelist? As far as I am concerned, they all are expounding the Word of God, with different titles and authoritative positions. The Bible say, too much is given, much is required.

Brothers and sisters don't let the secular world get along better in this area than we so called Christians or religious people do. We are supposed to be examples to the world. Not the world to us.

All of the women mentioned in this book will not be prophets. But, you will find a variety of categories and positions, some true and some false prophets, some women powerful, some great, some famous, and some not so powerful and famous, some as singers, writers, artist, builders, soldiers, some inventors and corporate leaders (CEO's). All receiving the knowledge they possess from our Father God, Almighty, according to **Deuteronomy 8:18.**

I will pour out my spirit upon all flesh, your sons and daughters shall prophesy. Joel 2:28

Acknowledgements

Kudos to my late grandmother Arlene McCullum, mother, Minnie Lee Martin, and spouse, Bishop Leon Sulton, and all of my family, sisters and brothers in Christ, that encouraged me in writing this book.

My grandmother hold the greatest impact in my life. She left the Church of God In Christ, and became an ordained Elder in the Church of God. She was in her Bible every free moment she had. I can visualize and yet hear her now. She would sit on her bed, read the word of God, seemingly amused at whatever she was reading, uttering statements to herself and I suppose to God in responding to whatever she had just read. Now as I read the Word of God, I too chuckle, and talk to Him, telling Him how wonderful and great He is to me.

I thank God for my former pastors that helped to mold me as well, and caused me to be what I am today. My formative years, we were under Pastor Baily in Ellisville,

I will pour out my spirit upon all flesh, your sons and daughters shall prophesy. Joel 2:28

Mississippi. My teen years into my young adult life was Pastor Arthur W. Goins, in New York City. Then we studied under Elder Cleveland Woods in Queens, all under that grand old Church of God in Christ, and later Pastor Winley of Soul Saving Station. My latter years, the late Bishop Leon Sulton which pushed me into becoming the pastor of Samuel's Temple COGIC, now I'm the Overseer of Samuel's Temple Deliverance Centers.

Bishop Sulton and my ordained mother with her Bachelor's Degree in Theology, Elder Minnie Martin, were my greatest boosters. Although I had the calling during the 70's, but refused to walk into it until my late husband insisted that it was time for me to step up to the leadership role. I've been moving forward ever since.

I want to thank my son Tyrone from Blue Box Entertainment for my promos, granddaughter Ashante for doing some research for me. Thank you granddaughter. And special kudos to my oldest grandson Rhamel for being my consultant. Thanks to my beautiful goddaughter Pastor Pricilla Wilson for the spelling of that French word cliché. Last but not least, my appreciations to Brother Bill Nadler for his great expertise.

I will pour out my spirit upon all flesh, your sons and daughters shall prophesy. Joel 2:28

Origin

This book will define to the best of my knowledge women from all walks of life.

PROMENANT WOMEN
COURAGEOUS WOMEN
OUTSTANDING WOMEN
DARING WOMEN
BRAVE WOMEN
WOMEN IN BATTLE
WOMEN PHROPHETES/
PREACHERS/True and False
OUTSTANDING WOMAN IN
THE SECULAR WORLD
PRAYFUL- POWERFUL and
PERSUASIVE WOMEN OF GOD
ALL
IN THE OLD and NEW TESTAMENTS
OUR HISTORY OF TODAY and YESTERYEAR

I will pour out my spirit upon all flesh, your sons and daughters shall prophesy. Joel 2:28

PART ONE

THE OLD TESTAMENT

Books of Law

Genesis

Exodus

Leviticus

Numbers

Deuteronomy

I will pour out my spirit upon all flesh, your sons and daughters shall prophesy. Joel 2:28

Women in the Books of Moses

I will pour out my spirit upon all flesh, your sons and daughters shall prophesy. Joel 2:28

Chapter 1

Viewpoints

There is so much controversy in the church world, concerning women in ministry, what they can and cannot or should not do. The secular world doesn't seem to have as many problems with this situation in today's society like that of the church world.

There is an abundant amount of work to be done to get people to enter into the kingdom of God. We really don't have time to debate over frivolous discussions, while thousands of boys and girls, men and women continue to die daily without being witnessed to in order to enter the kingdom of heaven, due to our negligence and misuse of the time God has entrusted in us. Many churches were initiated by women of both today, yesteryear, and in the Bible days. This is extremely evident in the New Testament through Paul's teaching.

I will pour out my spirit upon all flesh, your sons and daughters shall prophesy. Joel 2:28

I'm going to expound a little on what God has allowed me to have some insight on of His Word, as I study it daily on a continuous basis and not sporadic. I will approach this great controversy of women preachers with authority over men, through searching the scriptures.

According to the Old and the New Testaments, both allows us to see plainly women as preachers/prophetess, leaders, in battle, commanders, rulers, and many other positions also found in today's society of the twenty-first century, both giving authority over men and under the authority of men.

Food for thought, in the Old Testament, man brought woman into this world through God, in the New Testament woman brought man into this world through God. Galatians 4:4.

I will pour out my spirit upon all flesh, your sons and daughters shall prophesy. Joel 2:28

Chapter 2

Women in the Book of Genesis

Book One of Moses

Eve First Woman, Wife and Mother

In Genesis (the beginning), God spoke to Eve first concerning their sufferings after their sins, **Genesis 3:16-19.** "I will make your pain in child bearing very severe. With pain you will give birth to children. Then, He spoke to Adam. He told him," Because you listen to your wife, ate from the tree which I commanded that you should not eat of, "Cursed is the ground because of you, through pain and toil, and you will eat of it all the days of your life. It will produce thorns, and thistles for you, and you will eat plants

I will pour out my spirit upon all flesh, your sons and daughters shall prophesy. Joel 2:28

of the fields. By the sweat of your brow you will eat your food until you return to the ground."

Eve is the mother of all human beings. Eve was the first woman mentioned in the Bible **(Genesis 3:20, 4:1)**. She was created to be a compatible helper to Adam **(Genesis 2:18-22)**. Eve's sin of disobedience led us into great pain and sufferings during our childbirth. The scriptures put inferences on great pain as to say there would be pain, but not severe. Maybe the pain wouldn't be at all had they not sinned. Wouldn't it be wonderful to have pleasure with our spouse without the pain that comes with child bearing?

Sarah the Blessed

Women can make peace, cause war, destroy and save. They are powerful, in whatever they set out to do.

God promised Abraham in **Genesis Chapter 15,** to bless his seed. But they couldn't wait. Sarah decided to help God out. She gave Abraham permission to marry her maid Hagar. Abraham consented by marring her. Hagar became pregnant for him with Ishmael. This I suppose made Hagar feel superior over Sarah, due to her being barren. Now resentment set in. All hell broke loose. Sarah wants Hagar and the child to leave. There is no wrath like a woman's

I will pour out my spirit upon all flesh, your sons and daughters shall prophesy. Joel 2:28

wrath according to **Proverbs 21:9,** tells us that. It states that it is better to live on a corner of the rooftop, than to live in the house with a brawling woman. Hagar and Ishmael is an example of that. Sarah had Abraham to put them out! These are the kind of things that happens when we step in and try to help God out. Because we feel, He's not moving fast enough for us, we take matters into our own hands and cause a complete disaster. Hagar and her son, Abraham's seed, by his wife's slave, Hagar and her son Ishmael, was now sent into exile to die, all because Abraham and Sarah didn't wait on God to fulfill His promise.

Later in **Genesis 18:2,** Abraham was approached by three men which asked him for his wife Sarah. God didn't just promise Abraham the blessing, but He said "I will bless Sarah and give you a son by her. I will bless her so she will be the mother of nations; kings of people will come from her." He didn't leave her out of the blessing plan. God honored Sarah's thoughts and feelings just as he did Abraham's. For example when Abraham was told that they would have a child Sarah laughed because of her old age. That's why the scriptures ask, is there anything too hard for God? The answer is no! **Genesis 18:14.** Yes God included Sarah in the blessing plan too! Not only that, but through faith, He saw fit for her to be inducted in the Hall of Faith

I will pour out my spirit upon all flesh, your sons and daughters shall prophesy. Joel 2:28

Fame. **Hebrews 11:11**, Amen. *God never left women out of anything He did, from the beginning in Genesis to the end in Revelation, from followers to leadership. As a fact, it is said in the "**Judaism 101**: Prophets and Prophecy", the **Talmud** states that Sarah's Prophetic ability was superior to Abraham's.*

Now this is a revelation of shock. Not what was done, but the way it was done. This is the first time I saw it like this. That is Sarah told Abraham to get rid of Ishmael his son and Hagar the slave, because her son Isaac wasn't going to share heir with Ishmael, and God sanctioned it! He backed her up and told Abraham to listen to his wife and send them away! God told Abraham not to worry about Ishmael and Hagar because they were going to be blessed also. Ishmael would be ruler over a great nation of people as well. All these years I missed the part where Sarah told Abraham what to do and God agreed with her! Because Abraham's seed was going to be blessed through Sarah and their son Isaac and not Hagar with Ishmael. **Genesis 21:9-13.**

Another important fact in **Genesis chapter 21, verse 21**, is that Hagar chose a wife for her son Ishmael.

I will pour out my spirit upon all flesh, your sons and daughters shall prophesy. Joel 2:28

Lot's Daughters

Genesis 19:30, the Moabites and the children of Ammon, came about through two sisters raping their father Lot, after the destruction of the two cities, Sodom and Gomarrah. That was their way of a surety maintaining their father's seed for future generations to come. I would say that was to preserve their future generation, wouldn't you?

Rebekah

Genesis 27:5. Rebekah was the mother of twins, Jacob and Esau. During her pregnancy, prior to their birth, she realized a struggle was going on inside of her. She questioned God. God explained to her that she was carrying two nations. The older would serve the younger. So before their birth, Rebekah knew exactly what to expect. Therefore, at the first opportunity she got, she decided to help God out. Here again, when we interfere, we cause chaotic situations. Rebekah helped the younger son Jacob steal the birthright from the older son Esau. This caused Jacob to flee his home, thus alienating him from his immediate family. All because they didn't allow God to do it. Instead, Rebekah and Jacob took matters into their own hands, by doing it themselves.

I will pour out my spirit upon all flesh, your sons and daughters shall prophesy. Joel 2:28

7

Exodus – Book Two of Moses

Zipporah Saves Moses Life

We find in **Exodus 4:24-26,** that God met Moses in the place they were living at the time and was about to kill him. But Zipporah took a flint knife, cut off her son's foreskin and touched Moses' feet with it. Declaring him to be a bridegroom of blood to her. Therefore, the Lord let him alone. (At that time she used the phrase "bridegroom of blood," referring to circumcision.) God honored Zipporah's actions, she was able to save her husband's life by acting quickly and circumcised their son Eliezer. I don't believe she stopped to think, I'm a woman, and I better not do this thing. I believe her thoughts were to save her husband from death. This is the only scripture where I saw a woman practiced circumcision. She had to be in the right position to hear from God, how else would she know? Moses' life was spared by the hands of a woman's ingenuity and quick thinking.

I will pour out my spirit upon all flesh, your sons and daughters shall prophesy. Joel 2:28

Miriam as a Prime Leader and Prophetess

Miriam the oldest and sister of Aaron and Mosses, a prophetess, encourager, exalter, strong, and one of Israel's leaders, was sent by God to guide Israel. "For I brought thee up out of the land of Egypt, and redeemed thee out of the house of servants; and I sent before thee Moses, Aaron and Miriam" (**Micah 6:4**). Miriam was more than a great leader, she was a great palmist as well. She led Israel into great victorious victory songs of praise. I'm reminded of that great old Negro Spiritual song, "Go Down Moses, way down in Egypt land and tell old Pharaoh to let my people go." This is not a direct quote from the Bible but, it is believed that Miriam is the one that probably watched over her brother Moses when he was hid as an infant. Thus helping to raise her baby brother, now a powerful man of God, held in the hands of powerful women. First his mother, then his sister next Pharaoh's daughter. Remember the hands that rocks the cradle, rules the world.

Miriam was involved in a rebellion against her brother Moses, when he married an Ethiopian woman. She and her brother Aaron rebelled against Moses's leadership. Miriam was punished severely, she was struck with leprosy by God. Moses had to pray for her recovery. I believe she was

I will pour out my spirit upon all flesh, your sons and daughters shall prophesy. Joel 2:28

the initiator of the rebellion. She must have been mighty powerful for God to strike her and not Aaron.

Numbers – Fourth Book of Moses

Zelophehad's Five Daughters

In the book of **Numbers** we find the five brave powerful daughters of Zelophehad. They weren't timid, but bold, knew their rights and not afraid to speak up for them. Their father Zelophehad had no sons to pass down his inheritance to. Therefore his five daughters approached Moses, and Eleazar the priest, the leaders, prince, and all the congregation requesting the portion of land that belonged to their father. They felt strong about not being able to receive a portion of land thus being penalized because they were women. The distribution was among the brethren only. Moses took this matter to God in prayer. God told Moses, they are right. Give them their portion of the inheritance belonging to their father. The blessings are yet flowing down from the clan of Manasseh and Joseph his father, in this situation. Do you think they ruled over that property? Do you think it was only women living in those quarters? Yes

I will pour out my spirit upon all flesh, your sons and daughters shall prophesy. Joel 2:28

they ruled and no it didn't consist of women only, there were men as well under their leadership. They ruled and ruled well, yes Zelophehad's five daughters. Because of Zelophehad's daughters, the law was rewritten to read, if a man has no son, the inheritance is to be passed on to his daughter. This can be applied in many ways. For example, the church, woman can be leaders as well as men. There are qualified woman to be in the role of leadership as pastors. Here we have not one but five women in leadership for the Manasseh Clan. **Numbers 27:1-5.**

I will pour out my spirit upon all flesh, your sons and daughters shall prophesy. Joel 2:28

PART TWO

Books of History

Judges

Ruth

I Samuel

II Samuel

I Kings

II Kings

I Chronicles

II Chronicles

Ezra

Nehemiah

Ester

I will pour out my spirit upon all flesh, your sons and daughters shall prophesy. Joel 2:28

Chapter 3

Joshua – Sixth Book

Rahab the Prostitute

The book of Joshua was named after Joshua. Joshua was one of the two spies sent out by Moses to view the land they later conquered with the help of a woman by the name of Rahab, a prostitute.

Rahab was a woman of great faith. She believed in this great God she had heard so much about. All the miracles He had performed for the children of Israel, crossing the Red Sea, delivering them from the hands of Pharaoh, and destroying other nations for His people. She was a shero of her day and time. Her greatness landed her in the Hall of Faith and Fame, found in the book of **Hebrews 11:31.** She is also mentioned in two other books of the Bible in the New

I will pour out my spirit upon all flesh, your sons and daughters shall prophesy. Joel 2:28

Testament. **Matthew 1:5** as a lineage and **James 2:25**, as a shero.

It seems that Rahab initiated everything. She was reminded by the spies that she was the one that made the agreement or oath. She was the one who made them swear. Therefore if anything went wrong, she would be the cause of it. She used her persuasive powers, believing and knowing what God could do. This great woman used her faith in the God of Israel to save her family. Not only did she save her family but she was instrumental in the victory of the Israelites, an entire nation. She knew from past history that their land would be given into the hands of the Israelites. Therefore she bargain with Joshua's messengers, sent to spy. I will help you win this battle, just promise the safety of my family.

I view this as two fold. The men saved Rahab's family, but an entire nation of people was victorious by the hands of a woman. Yes! God used this woman, Rahab, a prostitute, to accomplish His goals and win the battle. Amen. **Joshua 2:1**

I will pour out my spirit upon all flesh, your sons and daughters shall prophesy. Joel 2:28

Judges – Seventh Book

Achsah

Achsah was the only daughter of Caleb. Caleb gave her away to Othniel, his nephew, the warrior which was victorious in taking the city of Kirjath-sepher. Why mention her? Because she was brave enough to ask for a blessing from her father that consist of springs of water to go with the land her father had given to them. She was a woman of wisdom. What good is land without water? Which means to me that she was an independent woman, full of wisdom, able to think for herself without depending solely on her now husband. She had knowledge, and understanding. She was more than brave, she was courageous. **Judges 1:12-15.**

Deborah the Judge/Prophetess-Preacher/Woman in Battle

God use whom and what He please, when and how He chose, where ever He want. In the Old Testament, He used a donkey, in the New Testament, He used a roster. He used David as a child and Deborah as a woman. Just

I will pour out my spirit upon all flesh, your sons and daughters shall prophesy. Joel 2:28

like Goliath was fooled by the lad David, I'm sure Sisera was fooled by the woman, Jael that lead to his demise. God does what He wants to do, when and how He wants to do it. Yes Deborah a woman, a deliverer, mother of Zion in Israel, a wife had given hope, peace and freedom to a rebellious stiff necked people that once again forgot about their Lord God Almighty. They forgot how He had delivered them out of the wilderness into the Promised Land. God promised Moses He would raise up prophets. He did, He raised up Judge Deborah to free His people once again from the Canaanites. Although they turned their backs on Him, living an adulterous, wicked idolatrous, and sinful life. But through God's love for them, once again he would deliver them through the hands of women.

In my studies on women preachers and leaders such as Deborah with authority over the nation of the Israelites, I decided to research the word Judge. Webster Dictionary gave several meanings, which are all excellent in their descriptions. One meaning was "to pass sentence upon; condemn, another was to determine or decide authoritatively after deliberation, to govern; rule, a <u>leader</u> of the Israelites for about four hundred years. It went on to describe the word Judge as a noun which denotes a person that's empowered to make decisions that determine points and issue".

I will pour out my spirit upon all flesh, your sons and daughters shall prophesy. Joel 2:28

It was Deborah, the fifth Judge of Israel. She was that powerful and mighty judge of Israel. She ruled the entire nation of Israel as a Judge, not a tribe, but all twelve tribes. She was instrumental in their peace for forty years **(Judges 4:5).** I determined that she ruled for forty years. Her leadership status was equivalent to that of our president for the United States of the Americans, as opposed to a Mayor for a city or governor for the state. She was married to Lapidoth. God spoke to Judge Deborah, and she responded immediately. He raised her up for such a time as this. To deliver His people, once again. She summoned Barak the general, and told him, that the Lord God of Israel commanded him to go (giving him orders from God, Deborah a woman) against Sisera with only ten thousand troops while Sisera had a multitude of troops and 900 iron chariots. God works with small numbers. Sisera had terrorized Israel for twenty long hard (20) years. Barak was afraid. Barak refused to go without being accompanied by Judge Deborah, thus showing a lack of strong male leadership. Deborah explained to him that she would go with him in the battle, but the Lord would hand the battle over to a woman and not a man. God sent deliverance for Israel through the hands of a WOMAN, through the faith of

I will pour out my spirit upon all flesh, your sons and daughters shall prophesy. Joel 2:28

a woman, leadership of a woman. Yes Deborah was a preacher, a woman, a ruler, with triumph and VICTORY for her people. All this done through the leadership of who? A woman named Deborah.

This victory isn't complete without mentioning other woman in the same chapter as Deborah, one named Jael, she is the shero, wife of Heber. While Barak sought after Sisera, Jael was the shero that killed him, and delivered him dead into his hands. Again at the hands of a shrewd and cleaver woman which lured Sisera in with kindness, a glass of milk, a large tent nail and a hammer. Just think had he awaken while she was in the process of trying to kill him. No, God was in the plan, she a woman, delivered him into the hands of Barak a man, dead. Hurrah for women used by God to win the battle. **Judges 4:15-22**. Jael was praised and went down in Bible history as a blessed woman, above all the woman of her tent, for her military and courageous acts.

Please know that the above battle, and all of the victories, mentioned in this book, was won by our mighty God, Lord and Savior. But, He choose to do it through the hands of women.

I will pour out my spirit upon all flesh, your sons and daughters shall prophesy. Joel 2:28

Manoah's Wife/Sampson's Mother

The entire **13th chapter of Judges** evolves around God's angel speaking directly to Manoah's wife. The Bible doesn't state why she was the one God dealt with initially, neither does it say where Manoah was at the time. However, it does state that she was in the field. But it is crystal clear that the angel dealt with her, and that she was the one the news was originally given to. Manoah received the revelation from his wife. The angel let Manoah know that he had given his wife the specifics for both her and the child's care.

I don't know why so many women were nameless in the Bible, but, they were yet important. They were simply referred to as the woman, wise woman, foolish woman, or the wife of, etc. Although many weren't given names, instead a title of being a woman or wife, they were yet of great significance. They gave birth to great leaders, kings, deliverers, and prophets. Virgin Mary gave birth to our Lord and Savior Jesus Christ, the King of kings, and Lord of lords. Her cousin, Elizabeth, gave birth to John the Revelator, the fore-runner of Jesus Christ, John the Baptist.

God found it fitting to let Manoah's wife know, that although she was barren, she would now be giving birth to a son. Not just a son, but a very special son. A son born

I will pour out my spirit upon all flesh, your sons and daughters shall prophesy. Joel 2:28

21

to once again deliver the children of Israel, which had done wrong repeatedly in the sight of God. The name of that great son was Sampson, recorded in the Bible as the strongest man ever lived. The Lord whispered this into my ear too. "Not only was Sampson's training set into motion before he was born, but before he was even conceived". Wow, what a revelation. Shouldn't be a surprised, because He told Jeremiah, "I knew you before I formed you in your mother's womb", **Jeremiah 1:5.** One more nugget, Manoah's wife was told what she shouldn't eat and drink during her pregnancy.

Now listen to this. When Manoah asked the Lord for the man of God to return, (not knowing that it was an angel), God listened to Manoah, but instead of approaching Manoah, he returned again to Manoah's wife! This was strictly an opportunity for the angel to speak to Manoah, because he was the one who made the request. However, he reappeared again to the wife. When the angel returned to her, she then ran and got her husband. Manoah asked God to teach them how to train their child. How many of us in today's society, ask God to lead and teach us how to train our children? They were given specific orders on how to nurture this child. The angel told Manoah, that these special orders were given to his wife on how to bring up their child. And that they were to follow the instructions

I will pour out my spirit upon all flesh, your sons and daughters shall prophesy. Joel 2:28

exactly as given. Which let me know, we are to pay close attention to the upbringing of our children, God's way and not ours. We too are given specific orders on training our children of today. That is to say, we should train them to be children of God, to be used by God, trained in God, to be spiritual leaders, such as pastors, elders, prophets, bishops, etc. Train them to be children fit for the kingdom, according to **Deuteronomy 6th** chapter, and many other instructional scriptures in the Bible. God has given us the formula, all we need to do is use it.

We as Christians should pay close attention to this particular chapter in the Bible. I feel that we have missed the meaning of it. Why do I say this? Because most all of my church life, the focus was on Sampson's strength and how he was beguiled by his wife Delilah, into revealing his secret of where his strength lies. The Lord imparted with me an additional meaning of this chapter. I'm convinced that it is to show us the importance of bring up our children in the admiration of the Lord. I've watched church parents rave over their little ones being able to dance to secular music. Not only do they dance to the music, but they know all the lyrics and tunes to the songs. They also encourage their offspring to indulge in secular music, with the hopes of them making it big, or maybe I should say becoming a star.

I will pour out my spirit upon all flesh, your sons and daughters shall prophesy. Joel 2:28

Our Bible provide us with many great mothers and fathers, that trained their children to be **g r e a t** men and women of God. You will find many of them mentioned throughout this book. Remember behind every great man is a great woman and behind every great woman is a great man. Imagine how pleased God will be with us, performing in His will, being a blessed and virtuous woman and a righteous man. **Proverbs 31:10-31**

In summation, God ministered to Manoah's wife through the angle. She ministered to her husband what was imparted to her. Israel was sent a savior through the great woman of God. The child Sampson, born to both Manoah and his wife, with the purpose to once again, save God's chosen people the Israelites from those bad people called the Philistines.

The Woman of Thebez

Abimelech killed all seventy of his brothers to assure his position as King. He was instrumental in seizing the city of Thebez. But he made a mistake, and pursued the men and women of Thebez up to a tower of safety and met his death.

Abimelech was killed by a certain woman. I would like to believe she was a woman of high standing, a special woman.

I will pour out my spirit upon all flesh, your sons and daughters shall prophesy. Joel 2:28

For the mere fact the writer put it as a certain woman. The certain woman cracked Abimelech's skull open with a millstone. She dropped it on his head from the tower. He didn't see it coming, especially from a woman.

Abimelech didn't want it to be said he was killed by a woman, what a pity. Therefore he called his armor bearers and commanded that they spear him to his death. **Judges 9:50-53.**

That woman of The'bez was so important that God saw fit for her to be mentioned again in **II Samuel 11:21.**

Yes, Abimelech a great warrior, killed by the power of a courageous woman, full of wisdom, the weaker vessel, with an enormous stone. Hurrah for a quick thinking woman that again saved a nation of people, the people of God. Just one woman. God work in small numbers to no numbers at all Amen.

I will pour out my spirit upon all flesh, your sons and daughters shall prophesy. Joel 2:28

Chapter 4

Ruth - Eight Book of the Bible

The book of Ruth is the most romantic love story ever told. A dedicated woman to her mother-in-law. She learned to serve the same God as Naomi. Later Ruth found her a good thing, her husband, Boaz. Through this union, came Obed. Through Obed King David, and through King David, our Lord and our Savor Jesus Christ. **Ruth 4:18-22.**

You will find the book of Ruth to be sentimental, sad, joyful, and spiritual. God chose Ruth, a heathen woman to be in the genealogy of our King Jesus and King David. God takes from the bottom and brings it up to the top. God takes nothing and turns it into something. Ruth is the prime example of such.

Ruth is the seventh book of the Old Testament. She is a chosen woman of God, in both the Old and New

I will pour out my spirit upon all flesh, your sons and daughters shall prophesy. Joel 2:28

Testaments. The book of Ruth is named and dedicated to her. She is mentioned in the first book of the New Testament. It acknowledge Ruth, as a devoted woman of God. Once a heathen, now a part of the linage of our Lord and Savior Jesus Christ. Look at what God can do! Amen. **Matthew 1: 5-17.**

I will pour out my spirit upon all flesh, your sons and daughters shall prophesy. Joel 2:28

Chapter 5

I Samuel – Ninth Book of the Bible

Hanna – mother of Samuel

The book of First Samuel consist of thirty-one chapters. The first two are mostly concerning Hanna the mother of Samuel, before and after he was born. Samuel's name has several meanings. A few meanings are: asked of God, heard of God, and God's heart. Samuel grew up to be a great prophet of God. He crowned Saul and David as kings. He was the last of the judges that ruled Israel before they had kings.

Samuel was born to a heart broken, spirit filled, wealthy, praying, and faith believing woman of God, named Hanna, with a loving husband. Hanna had the best of all worlds, she was blessed but barren. Elkanah, Hanna's husband was

I will pour out my spirit upon all flesh, your sons and daughters shall prophesy. Joel 2:28

a wealthy man, and had great love for her, more than he did for his second wife that bare him children. Due to the fact that Hanna was unable to give birth to children, Peninnah the second wife, poked fun at her. I'm sure this made her feel unworthy and less than a woman. It sent Hanna into a sorrowful state of mind, crying, abstaining from eating and bitter towards her adversary.

Therefore, Hanna suffering pain and agony sent her laments and petition before her God. Not only did she pour her soul out while praying, but she made a vow to the Lord. The vow, if God gave her a son, she would give it back to Him for life. How many of us have given our children to the Lord God? Hanna was willing to give up her child to God, to show her gratitude for honoring her prayer through the opening of her womb. She followed **Deuteronomy 26** admonishing us to teach and train our children, put signs on the door post, platelets on our four heads etc. Are we training our children? Are we giving them back to God? I've watched parents entice children to practice worldly dances, sing worldly songs and many other things instead of training them the way they should go as our Bible have instructed us to do. Another form of training and the greatest is being an example. Don't let our children see us do things, hear us say things that's not pleasing to God. Children mimic what

I will pour out my spirit upon all flesh, your sons and daughters shall prophesy. Joel 2:28

they see adults do. They catch on very quick to non-positive things and stuff. In my observation, children seem to have a sense of right and wrong at an early age of infancy. They practice on us and wait for our response.

God blessed Hanna with a male child, just what she prayed for. God kept His promise to Hanna, and she didn't forget her vow to Him either, as so many of us do. She blessed God, thanked God, praised God and rejoiced in Him for His mighty and wonderful work of blessing her with a child, a male child, a son Samuel.

Hanna reframed from going to the temple with the child until he was old enough to be on his own. She explained to her husband that she would not go to the house of God until the child was able to remain there at the temple forever without his parents. Elkanah Hanna's husband, was a man of understanding, a man of God, he didn't question her, instead he believed and trusted her. His response was, do whatever you feel is right. Wait until the child is old enough to leave and keep your vow to OUR God. We need a few Elkanahs and Hannahs around today. What a strong, out spoken powerful, woman of faith in God. Hanna took time and trained Samuel as instructed in **Deuteronomy 6:6-9**.

In the training of our children, we should have devotion before they leave the house, or before we leave our homes

I will pour out my spirit upon all flesh, your sons and daughters shall prophesy. Joel 2:28

daily, thus training them in the Word of God. We depend on the world to train our children. We have failed to use our parental rights shaping and molding them into godly beings.

Through the early training of Samuel he was able to minister before God as a <u>young</u> child. Hanna even dressed him in proper attire. She girded him with a linen Ephod. Attire fitting his position as a prophet. I watch parents dress their children completely different to what the Word of God has instructed us to do. Halloween is a prime example. We dress them as Batman, Cinderella, and all the worldly characters children like to imitate and or idolize. I know we all don't participate in such activity. But I have yet to see one dressed as a preacher, ha ha! Do your child poses a Bible? We run out and buy them all kinds of educational books, to increase their scholastic education and games to entertain them. Yes, you might have a children's Bible with some notable Bible characters in it. Might! Do your child or children see you reading your Bible daily? Or once a week in church? Nowadays people are using their cell phones and I-pads to read the Word of God in CHURCH y'all! They don't even bring their Bibles to church anymore.

I'm so sorry I didn't have a better understanding at an early age to call those things as if though they are. Meaning, let us label our children as prophets, bishops, evangelist,

I will pour out my spirit upon all flesh, your sons and daughters shall prophesy. Joel 2:28

great men and women of God. Some parents do, but they live a shabby life as far as being an example. I hear parents training them to be doctors, lawyers, etc. Guess what? Our children can obtain and learn to live a godly life through training in our homes and through us for free. All it require is time spent with God and our children. God has given us specific formulas in Deuteronomy, Ephesians and Ecclesiastes. All we have to do is take it and run with it, He will do the rest.

Samuel, a leader of Israel, man of God, major prophet, came through the prayers of a faith believing, blessed woman of God, named Hannah. **I Samuel 1:1-28.**

Abigail

Abigail was the wife of Nabal. He was an extremely wealthy man, a leader with a beautiful wife. She was well educated and full of wisdom. She didn't wait around as a weakling woman, waiting to see what might happen after her husband had dealt so wickedly with King David. She was a woman of faith that dared to step out into the world of miracles, knowing that God would intervene. Abigail was strong. She took the leadership role or maybe I should say the initiative and reached out to King David with bravery,

I will pour out my spirit upon all flesh, your sons and daughters shall prophesy. Joel 2:28

after her evil husband had played the role of a fool, and belittled David's men, to save herself and their people.

What did she do? After hearing how well David had treated their wealthy possessions of cattle and men, and how Nabil refused David's request for help with a little food instead he played the fool. Pretending he didn't have any knowledge of David, disregarding his fame that went throughout the entire land. Abigail didn't acknowledge her husband in this matter. She knew that they were in deep trouble. Yes, it had triggered David into destroying Nabal and all of his people. But Abigail went forefront, she took the lead, rushed to meet the King, a great warrior, not empty handed but took some victuals and bottles of wine to him. Thus sparing her life and the lives of her people.

What a brave, wise, and courageous woman. Later, it landed her into being the wife of the King. King David called her as a blessed woman, sent by God. **I Samuel 25:1-44.**

Woman of Tekoah

Women are effective in whatever they set out to do, good or bad. This is evident in the woman of Tekoah. Joab wanted a message to be sent to the king in an effective way.

I will pour out my spirit upon all flesh, your sons and daughters shall prophesy. Joel 2:28

So he looked for a WOMAN, full of wisdom to do the job. **II Samuel 14**:4-24. Was he successful in finding such a woman? Sure he was, the woman of Tekoah.

The Woman knew how to get the attention of the king. She fell on her face, giving obeisance, posing as a mourner. She was an attention getter. Help, O king! She cried. What's wrong? He answered immediately, after that Grammy Award performance she had given. Now the stage was set. She had all of his attention. Now she would deliver Joab's message to King David.

Next, she painted a sorrowful picture in his mind, of her being a widow, husband dead, strife between her sons, and one son killing the other. Now the entire family had turned against her, a poor widow. Because they are ready to kill the other son for killing his brother, thus eradicating her husband's name. Yes, she has the king right where she wanted him to be. He is willing to protect her from any danger. However, all of this was done on behalf of the king's son Absalom, lonesome for his family and wanting to return home from his flight after the murder of his brother.

Joab accomplished his mission through the woman of Tekoah. Absalom could now return home to his family.

I Samuel 18:6-7, It was the women that came out from all of the cities jamming with musical instruments,

I will pour out my spirit upon all flesh, your sons and daughters shall prophesy. Joel 2:28

tambourines, dancing and singing, sending up great praises of celebration for King Saul and King David. However, they praised King David more than King Saul, causing jealousy to set up in King Saul. I believe the song went like this because the Bible states that the women answered in the song. The question was this, "How many did Saul kill and how many did David kill?" The answer was this, "Saul has slain his thousand, and David his ten thousand".

A Wise Woman

Why? I don't know, but many woman were used in great victories in the Old Testament, without a name. In most cases, they were the cause of the Victory. For example, **II Samuel 20:16-22**, a wise woman approaches Joab as being a peaceful and faithful woman in Israel. She prevented a city from being destroyed by delivering the head of She'ba, the man that threaten King David's life. What did she do? She was successful in getting all the people together, beheaded She'ba, and delivered his head, thrown over the wall. She had leadership qualities, wouldn't you agree? Not only did she have those qualities, but she exercised them.

I will pour out my spirit upon all flesh, your sons and daughters shall prophesy. Joel 2:28

Chapter 6

Bathsheba

I can't speak for anyone else, but I often wondered why it doesn't show where Bathsheba resisted King David's lustful desire he had for her. I believe she welcomed it. The king? That's just like our president approaching one of us. We being nowhere near his status of being in the company of the president of the United States of America. She must have sent some strong signals out. Powerful enough to lure the king into having an affair, murdering her husband, then end up being his wife, and bore a powerful son, King Solomon. He ruled as one of the greatest kings ever. Filthy rich and full of wisdom during his leadership.

Bathsheba showed her greatest strength in getting her son into his rightful position as king, after Nathan told her that Adonijah, Solomon's brother was being prompted into being the next king, she got busy. Bathsheba went to King David

I will pour out my spirit upon all flesh, your sons and daughters shall prophesy. Joel 2:28

and reminded him of his promise for their son Solomon, to be the next king, sitting on the throne.

Almighty God always seem to work miracles, and cause victorious battles with a few, rather than large numbers. He used Nathan the prophet, Zadok the priest, Benaiah, Solomon and Bathsheba. However, they weren't invited to the celebration of Adonijah. Adonijah invited the entire host of the children of Israel to his grand celebration of kingship. All of the King's sons, Abithar the priest, and captains, celebrating his Kingman ship, with abundance of fine foods and wine.

I believe Bathsheba knew how to get a prayer through. Because after Nathan the prophet counseled with her, next, she and Nathan, conferred with King David. Then things began to be set into motion immediately. Preparations were made, they had a closed private ceremony. King David had Zadok the priest and Nathan the prophet anoint Bathsheba's son to be King Solomon from the bed side of the great King David.

Although King David was old and feeble, he was strong in his mental capacity. He kept his promise to Bathsheba and Solomon. He was yet powerful. This lead me to believe what Bathsheba want, Bathsheba get. What a powerful woman! **I Kings 1:1-53.**

I will pour out my spirit upon all flesh, your sons and daughters shall prophesy. Joel 2:28

We have another encounter with Adonijah and his mother Haggith, and Solomon with his mother Bathsheba. If you can't get in one door, try another. That's exactly what Adonijah did in a very short time, after the death of King David, their father.

Adonijah approached Bathsheba concerning the kingship being taken from him and given to his brother Solomon. Now rightfully so, it belonged to Adonijan age wise, in man's eye sight, since he was the eldest. But God saw fit for it to be given to Solomon.

Again Bathsheba interacts between Adonijah and now, King Solomon. She delivers the message from Adonijah to King Solomon. His request was that King Solomon give him Abishag to wife. Now Abishag was the young nurse hired to try and revive King David during his old age, but unsuccessful. However, Solomon saw this as a threat to his kingship. Little did Adonijah know, he had written his death ticket! King Solomon had Adonijah killed. **I Kings 2:13-25.**

Queen of Sheba

Here again is a famous woman in the scriptures without a name. She was a famous Queen, a business woman, wealthy, a female leader of an entire nation of people of the

I will pour out my spirit upon all flesh, your sons and daughters shall prophesy. Joel 2:28

south in her country, a ruler with full authority and hired staff. She had to be a woman full of knowledge, in order to ask King Solomon such hard and tough questions of knowledge, which meant she was a person full of wisdom as well, in order to ask questions that only King Solomon could answer, **I kings 10:1-13.**

The Queen of Sheba was worth mentioning by our Lord and Savior Jesus Christ in the New Testament as well. She will rise up and condemn this wicked generation as one of the judges at the return of Jesus Christ our Lord and Savior **Matthew 12:42**. Now that's powerful.

Jezebel

Just like we have good and bad male leaders, we have good and bad female leaders. Jezebel the daughter of a King, a Queen, a prophetess, famous, woman full of authority, a leader, but corrupt, full of evil, and a murderer. She was a prime example of a wicked female leader. She conspired against God's prophets, worshipped idols, and false gods. She turned an entire city into idol worshippers of Baal. **First Kings 18, 19, and First Kings 20.** All of the prophets which stood for righteousness had to be careful, for fear of

I will pour out my spirit upon all flesh, your sons and daughters shall prophesy. Joel 2:28

their lives in danger. For the wicked woman Jezebel sought after the prophets of God to kill them.

One wicked deed performed was when King Ahab, Queen Jezebel's husband wanted Naboth's property. But Naboth refused to trade or sell his family's inheritance. For this Queen Jezebel orchestrated a plan to take it. And that she did. She put on a fast, forged her husband's name on letters of lies to decree the death of Naboth. She conspired using false witnesses and evidence against him that caused him to lose his life. All because he wouldn't trade nor sell his family's inheritance to her husband, King Ahab. What was he accused of? Jezebel claimed that Naboth spoke evil of God and the King. Therefore, she lied and had him murdered, then gave his property to her husband. What a wicked woman. Those type of actions yet exist today. People will take over what's rightfully yours. Then leave you to die. If it was at all possible, I would be spiritually dead, for the lies people have told on and about me. I thank God, He has kept me through it all. **I Kings 21**

King Ahab, the husband of Jezebel repented, but his wife, Queen Jezebel remained wicked until the dreadful day of her assignation. As a result of her non repenting heart, she was thrown from her window, where she plunged to her death without a proper burial. Her body was eaten, as

I will pour out my spirit upon all flesh, your sons and daughters shall prophesy. Joel 2:28

prophesied by Prophet Elijah the Tishbite. Yes, she died in her evil and wicked ways. A King's daughter, and a King's wife, died without anything she could be identified by! **II Kings 9:30-37.**

A Great Woman in Shunem

II Kings 4:8-37. This great no name prayerful woman of authority, a Shunammite woman of God living in Shunem, seem to be a spokesman for her household as well as a seer and woman in charge. This woman perceived that Elisha was a holy man of God which deserved to be treated with special care. Therefore she shared this with her husband, suggesting that he be given royal care, with his own room to lodge and food to eat during his travels. Through her blessing the man of God lead to a great blessing for her from God through His prophet Elisha.

Prophet Elisha perceived that she was childless and promised her the blessing of a son. This must have been a prayer she probably prayed for many years during her married life, because her husband was old. Now this great miracle is about to happen. The Shunammite woman is promised a child, a male child, although married to a man of old age. Notice that the Bible didn't state she was barren,

I will pour out my spirit upon all flesh, your sons and daughters shall prophesy. Joel 2:28

but her husband was old. Maybe too old for his seed to be fruitful. But there is nothing too hard for God.

God seem to get pleasure in blessing the old and childless couples with children in their old age during the Bible days. The Bible states that he was old. It seems to elude the fact that she was much younger than her husband. She was a woman of high standing, well respected, in charge. To give more clarity, she was a woman in authority. I like the way the Shunammite woman is portrayed in the book of **Second Kings, fourth chapter.** The husband is mentioned in the beginning and the middle, but the wife takes the lead role and is mainly focused on all the way through from the eight to the thirty-seventh verse, which lead me to believe she was highly respected and looked up to among her people.

The prophecy becomes true, a son is born. He develops into a young man, and took ill while helping his father during harvest time. The father sends the sick son home to his mother. While there with his mother, he dies on her knees. Faith caused her to lay him on Prophet Elisha bed. She summonsed her husband, asking for a young boy and a horse to take her to the man of God. He didn't have the faith she possessed, therefore he questioned whether or not it was the right thing to do. All is well she said. What a great story. She commanded the young man to drive as swift as he

I will pour out my spirit upon all flesh, your sons and daughters shall prophesy. Joel 2:28

could, don't slow, don't' slack, nor stop for anything unless she bade him. After reaching the man of God, her faith stretched a little further. She reminded the prophet of her not wanting to be deceived, thinking she was going to have a male child. Now that she was blessed with him, he was dead. What was she to do? God worked another miracle through the man of God. Once again, she was given her son, his life was restored through the same prophet Elisha.

Four chapters later, the **eight chapter of II Kings**, starting at **verse one**, Prophet Elisha encounters the same woman he met in Shunem again. This time he summons her and her household to leave their now dwelling place with the Philistines. Because God had showed him there was going to be a seven year famine. So she obediently returned to her home town in Shunem. I wonder why Prophet Elisha didn't give these instructions to the husband. Maybe because he was way old by now, or perhaps deceased. She did have a husband in chapter four and it did state that he was old. It seems that she honored and respected him to the highest. She was sure to inform him of every detail concerning her whereabouts in the fourth chapter. Another clue that she was in full charge, is that she and her whole household relocated under her auspices or maybe I should say her directives. This

I will pour out my spirit upon all flesh, your sons and daughters shall prophesy. Joel 2:28

is what I gleaned from reading about the great Shunammite woman in Shunem.

Athaliah

II Kings chapter eleven, we have another wicked woman, in charge, by the name of Queen Ataliah. She had power, and utilized it to the utmost, in order to gain leadership over Judah. Athaliah's father was Ahab, the husband of Jezebel. Maybe she learned her devious ways from her supposedly mother Jezebel. The Bible isn't clear whether her mother was Jezebel or not. However, it does show that her hunger and thirst for being the ruler after the death of her son Ahaziah, lead her to assonate all seventy sons of the royal seed, which was her own flesh and blood, and her grandsons. She thought she had murdered all! One, Joash was left, hide in the house of God, by his aunt, King Ahazian's sister. God will hide us from the enemy, if we serve Him, Amen. Athaliah the grandmother, murdered all seventy of her grandsons, the royal seed, because she didn't want anyone standing in the way or her ruling over Judah. It goes to show you, some people will do anything to gain power.

I will pour out my spirit upon all flesh, your sons and daughters shall prophesy. Joel 2:28

After the death of her son Ahaziah, she ruled Judah for six years, before she was murdered in the same like manner she herself had committed.

Huldah an Educator/Wife and Preacher

Huldah a Preacher, a wife, a Professor and the proprietor of her College, was sought after by King Josiah, Priest Hilkiah and others to break down the Words in the book of the Law of God they found in the house of God and had not obeyed it. Yes she was an educator, a leader, woman of God, and an entrepreneur. This powerful woman had her own College, a wife, a preacher, and a professor, the CEO, where learning went on in a coed manner. She had knowledge to the highest degree, both natural and spiritual, right in the Old Testament. Not only that, but she wasn't threatened by the five top men including the priest, that approached her for her counseling concerning the Word of God, neither were they threaten by her scholastic and pedagogical background. Wow, what a great God we serve. We have not because we ask not.

God's chosen people had stopped reading the Word of God and began to worship false gods, thus committing idolatry. Huldah had a word direct from God. She didn't

I will pour out my spirit upon all flesh, your sons and daughters shall prophesy. Joel 2:28

hold anything back, she spoke boldly with authority, and told it just like our Lord God said it. The message to the king from God through the woman of God was that evil was about to overtake Juda because they had forgotten their God. They had turned their backs on Him and began to worship false gods. But because of the tender heart and humble spirit of King Josiah, concerning the Words in the book. God promised that King Josiah would not encounter any of His wrath towards the children of Juda. He would refrain, until after King Josiah went to his grave and rest in peace.

There was a young woman by the name of Sherah, a descendant of Ephraim, found in **I Chronicles 7:24**. She is noted for building and fortifying three villages, Lower Beth-Horon, the nether, Upper Beth-Horon and Uzzen Sherah. I would say she was a builder, wouldn't you?

Prophetess Huldah is mentioned in both **II Kings 22:1 and II Chronicles 34:22-28 and II Chronicles 35:20-27.**

II Chronicles 35:20-27, lets us know that judgement did fall upon Judah as prophesied by the prophetess. However, King Josiah didn't die in peace because of his refusal to adhere to Neco's request for him to forebear, so he wouldn't be killed. He didn't take heed. Therefore he was killed.

I will pour out my spirit upon all flesh, your sons and daughters shall prophesy. Joel 2:28

Nuggets

These are nuggets and gyms to ponder on:

An old adage. The hand that rocks the cradle, rules the world.

My mother's wise words of wisdom were: If God can speak through a donkey to question his master, **Numbers 22:24-25**, and use a rooster **to** remind Peter that he would deny Jesus three times before the rooster crowed, **Matthew 26:57**. Having said that, God can certainly use a woman to carry His Word. And so He did. **Matthew 1:18-25, and Luke 2:1-7,** which tells us that Jesus the Son of God, was born of a woman, the Virgin Mary. If God wanted it to be so, Jesus could have been from a man, Eve was. She was taken from Adam's side. But the scriptures had to be fulfilled which the prophets of old had prophesied concerning Jesus entering this world in a physical being. That is Jesus Christ would be born of a virgin. God has no respect of person, He uses whom He please, when He please and for whatever purpose and where He please. Now catch this, Adam was made from dirt, and Jesus Christ was sent through the spirit of the Holy Ghost which allowed Mary a woman to conceive. Last but not least, "For with God, nothing shall be impossible **Luke 1:37**".

I will pour out my spirit upon all flesh, your sons and daughters shall prophesy. Joel 2:28

Chapter 7

Noadiah

Nehemiah was plotted against by an evil and false prophetess by the name of Noadiah, along with some false male prophets. She tried along with the male prophets to stop the work of God. No one can stop the work of God, no one! **Nehemiah 6:14**

The Book of Esther

In the Book of Esther, two types of characteristics are portrayed here, one godly and one ungodly. Queen Vashti the ungodly and Queen Ester the godly.

Queen Vashti was a beautiful woman. I'm sure she wanted for nothing. But probably because of her beauty and status as the Queen, she was a bit puffed up. Why do I say this? Because she refused her presence at the request

I will pour out my spirit upon all flesh, your sons and daughters shall prophesy. Joel 2:28

of the King at one of their most important festivals. This unacceptable behavior lead to her denunciation as the Queen. Not only did this show disrespect as the Queen towards the king, but other woman could become disrespectful as well. Not so much to their husbands, but to authority. This action led to opening the door for Esther becoming the next Queen and Vashti's demise. **Esther Chapter 1.**

Furthermore Queen Vashti defied the king, thus giving Esther the opportunity to be pronounced as Queen. For God had put her in place for such a time as this to save his nation of people, the Israelites. **Esther Chapter 2.**

The power of Queen Esther enabled her to lead her people in a victorious victory, as well as fasting and prayer. Also through her humility, she was able to get the attention of the King on the third day of the feast, at the request of her uncle Mordecai to join them in fasting and pray in saving their people.

The Book of Esther let us know that even though we may obtain high offices in this world, we cannot escape the calling of our Lord and Savior, although it could be as high as the White House, we are yet responsible for the salvation of the people.

I will pour out my spirit upon all flesh, your sons and daughters shall prophesy. Joel 2:28

Through the supplication of Queen Esther, her Uncle Mordecai and their people, the ones that sought after their lives became the victims of their own demise they sat for God's chosen people. Amen.

One might ask why include Queen Esther? I did because the Queen was extremely instrumental in saving her people. A whole nation of people saved, by being in the right place at the right time. It also indicates that yes men are the head, they are our superior, yet it doesn't state that women can't have authority, nor does it state that they can't be in charge with power that includes leadership. This is clearly seen in the book of Ester. She was a leader with power, wisdom and understanding. She was an orator, she made decisions, gave orders, commands and demands, an organizer with great insight, a woman of God that fasted and prayed. Esther was truly a powerful and great leader. She was a shero of her day and time.

Again here is a man, her Uncle, Mordecai which depended on the authority and power of a woman, for the salvation of their people, the Jews. And salvation it was, even to the elevation of Mordecai given the highest position that could be obtained except it be the King. He was next to the King!

I will pour out my spirit upon all flesh, your sons and daughters shall prophesy. Joel 2:28

PART THREE

Books of Poetry

Job
Psalms
Proverbs

Ecclesiastes
Song of Solomon

I will pour out my spirit upon all flesh, your sons and daughters shall prophesy. Joel 2:28

Chapter 8

A Virtuous Woman

Proverbs 31:10-31, is a well-known and familiar scripture which woman loved to harp on when trying to make a point about women preachers and so on, as far as I can remember during my youth.

This portion of scripture doesn't show that this virtuous woman was a prophetess, however, it does show that she was a woman of God, with high integrity and a well-known business woman among both men and women able to make sound decisions. I particular love the way it begins with a question, "Who can find a virtuous woman?" I contend, what is a virtuous woman? According to the Bible, the description of a virtuous woman is a woman that can be trusted by her husband, she does good towards him and not evil, there's no price tag on her, she arise early and meet the merchants, she's self-employed as opposed to staying home

I will pour out my spirit upon all flesh, your sons and daughters shall prophesy. Joel 2:28

waiting on her husband to bring home the bacon, not only that but, she makes sure the entire household have food to eat, she's an entrepreneur that knows how to purchase and market her merchandise, she looks out for the poor and needy, she is brave and gets the best for her household, she is strong and is honored, she's never idle, she's full of wisdom and kindness, her children and husband praise her and call her blessed, because of her, her husband is well known, her husband the CEO (Chief Executive Officer), and she is the COO (Chief of Operations), of her business. Last, but not least, she is a great leader and woman of God, full of wisdom and power. Her works will speak for themselves in the gates of heaven. Amen.

My take on this, is that this woman of God is hard to find in these days. We do good to find a woman that's doing half of this let alone all of it. I'm out of breath just reading through it, picture doing it. However, if we as women would take this portion of scripture and try to abide by it, I believe it would help to shape our children into a more productive generation. Saying that to say this again, the hand that rocks the cradle, rules the world.

I will pour out my spirit upon all flesh, your sons and daughters shall prophesy. Joel 2:28

A Bitter Woman

Ecclesiastes 7:26, examines how bitter a woman can be. It classifies her bitterness more severe than death. We feel death is the ultimate, not according to Solomon. He states that a woman's bitterness is worse than death. The ungodly woman will set snares and nets to catch you in. That is if you are not godly, and seeking the things of righteousness to please God. The way of escape is through God and only God. This is one of the seven things King Solomon found out when he was seeking wisdom of what and why wickedness and foolishness occur.

My thoughts on this is, women let us not be bitter, no matter what the situation might be.

King Solomon and Women

Although this book is about women, I'm including King Solomon, whose mother was Bathsheba. Because she played an important role in his becoming the king.

King Solomon was surrounded by many women. He had three hundred concubines and seven hundred wives, that's a total of one thousand women all in his possessions. Now here is the kicker, he loved them and he listened to them, he

I will pour out my spirit upon all flesh, your sons and daughters shall prophesy. Joel 2:28

took their counsel and advice. The scriptures declares that they turned his heart away from God to burn incense and worship idol gods.

King Solomon's first signs of his God given wisdom shown, was exhibited when he dealt with two prostitute mothers, with two infant sons. **I Kings 3:16-28.** Both mothers had slept with their infants, one mother slept on her son and killed the child. They both claimed the living child. King Solomon solved the problem by threatening to split the living son into half, thus giving each mother a half. The true identity of the real mother came forth exclaiming that she would rather give it to the lying mother, so the child could live. The lying mother wanted it cut so neither would have a child. Thus the problem was solved of whom the real mother was.

I will pour out my spirit upon all flesh, your sons and daughters shall prophesy. Joel 2:28

PART FOUR

Major Prophets

Isaiah

Jeremiah

Lamentations

Ezekiel

Daniel

I will pour out my spirit upon all flesh, your sons and daughters shall prophesy. Joel 2:28

Chapter 9

A Virgin/Isaiah

Let's talk about that great prophet Isaiah and the record he left for us to examine. He prophesied that our Lord and Savior would be born through a virgin approximately seven hundred and fifty years prior to His birth. Who was that virgin seven hundred and fifty years later? Mary! Joseph's wife, the mother of Jesus Christ our Lord and Savior. Now this is not a simple matter, nor is to be taken light. This is a major event which took place seven hundred and fifty years later, after the prophecy that the Word of God would be entering this physical world through a woman! That's a blessing, an honor, a privilege, and most of all a miracle wrought by God Himself through the Virgin Mary. **Isaiah 7:1**

I will pour out my spirit upon all flesh, your sons and daughters shall prophesy. Joel 2:28

Isaiah's Wife/Isaiah

Isaiah speaks of his wife being a prophetess, a preacher, conceiving a male child by the name of Maher-shalel-hash-baz for him. A name given by God through him. We all know that Isaiah was a major prophet. It seems they both, he and his wife were prophets. I believe Isaiah and his wife were working together as a husband and wife team. Not only that but he was in high favor of it. Why do I say that? Because he's the one that let us know that she was a prophetess. Not only was he proud, but was also very boastful about it. Wow, what a major revelation**! Isaiah 8:3**

God Speaks to the Women through Prophet Isaiah

Isaiah 32:9 certainly should be applied to the women of today's society, just as it was to the women in Jerusalem then. As I often say, our Lord God has blessed us bountiful in this twenty-first century. So much so that we forgot about God, praying, and fasting. We've become so comfortable and satisfied in our wealth. Some of us have so many clothes, we don't know what to wear. Sometimes we have things with the tags still on them hanging in our closets for years, never looked at, let alone wear. We hoard things we'll never wear.

I will pour out my spirit upon all flesh, your sons and daughters shall prophesy. Joel 2:28

We have shoes and expensive jewelry to match every outfit. We have three or four different categories of clothes. Casual, business, dressy, formal wear, and gym clothes. I remember the times we had one Sunday's best and the weekly clothes made from burlap, and flower sacks. I said that to say this, God didn't bless us to store up stuff, sit in our fine homes and drive around in our fine cars and forget about his lost sheep. Instead, He want us to come down off of our high horses and be about our Father's business. Some of us sit around idle, nothing to do but watch the dumb box and gossip on the phone. God didn't bless us for that either. He blessed us to serve Him. We serve Him through serving others. In doing this we will have peace and experience great joy.

God is letting us know through His prophet Isaiah, that He wants us to be a holy people, righteous and spirit filled, otherwise we are headed down the wrong path to destruction. Amen. Isaiah was noted for addressing both men and women in the book of Isaiah. When he finished speaking to the men, he would then turn and addressed the women as well. Now we find this same pattern in the New Testament, practiced by Apostle Paul. He let the entire congregation both men and women know they had a responsibility for their own salvation. That responsibility

I will pour out my spirit upon all flesh, your sons and daughters shall prophesy. Joel 2:28

was to repent, turn from their wickedness and serve the Lord their God whole heartedly and not hypocritically.

Jeremiah Demands Help from the Women

Jeremiah was called by God before he was conceived according to the scriptures. God told Jeremiah to go and get those weeping women. Jeremiah was a weeper himself. He cried out, hey you woman, I need your help! All you woman that know how to weep. You know how to call out to God and get His attention. You know how to get a prayer through. Not only did Jeremiah make a plea for the women to weep for the transgressions of the people, but he wanted them to hurry up and help! Yes, he commanded the crafty, cunning and shrewd women to come and help immediately! I would say that Jeremiah knew the power that sincere women of God incubate. They don't stop until they've achieved what they believe to be. The theory is to pray until something happen.

What did they need help in doing? Once again Israel had turn their backs on God, forsaken His Law and refuse to be obedient. Therefore Jeremiah's plea was for the people to return to their Lord God in obedience to avoid destruction upon the land. Another reason why he called the weeping

I will pour out my spirit upon all flesh, your sons and daughters shall prophesy. Joel 2:28

women, is that they would be persistent until they got results in getting the attention of the Lord God. **Jeremiah 9:17-20.**

I would like to join Prophet **Isaiah 58:1** together with Prophet **Jeremiah 9:17-19.** Prophet Jeremiah said called for the weeping women while Prophet Isaiah said it in a different way, his plea was to "Cry loud spare not, lift up your voice like a trumpet, and show my people their transgressions, and the house of Jacob their sins". Both pleas are for the children of Israel to obey and turn back to God!

Jeremiah 31:22 states that "a woman shall compass a man". I studied, researched and meditated on this passage of scripture for a while to try and get the answer and or true meaning of "to compass a man". The question is what a compass is and for what purpose does it serve? Therefore, I conclude that we all know a compass is a device that encircles, give directions, and determines geographical directions. It consist of a magnetic needle or needles horizontal mounted or suspended with the freedom to pivot aligned with the magnetic field of the earth, according to Webster's Dictionary. So in spite of all the other interpretations and meanings I found, I came up with my own interpretation. However, I believe God gave it to me, because as I began to write from the prospective of others, I couldn't make the connection. As I begin to

I will pour out my spirit upon all flesh, your sons and daughters shall prophesy. Joel 2:28

write from Webster's Dictionary's meaning, my eyes were opened to have a better and a clearer insight according to the dictionary's meanings. Which guided me in my God given explanation.

Since the word compass has its meaning as to encircle, give directions etc. Now you see where I'm going? Okay, a woman shall compass a man, surround him, and determine directions in other words lead as she is led by our Lord and savior Jesus Christ, which is the magnet that draws and point to the directions we all should go. Remember a compass shows you the way to go. It leads you, steers you in the right direction to travel. Now since technology has kicked in, we have navigators to lead you walking or driving, we no longer need the compass. Jesus Christ is our navigator, which steers us into the right direction. All we have to do is follow His lead all the way from earth to glory. Hallelujah.

Ezekiel 13:17. In Ezekiel we find that God speaks to both female and male prophets. However, He specifically addresses the woman prophetess concerning their misrepresentation of Him. How His wrath is coming on them for their false interpretation and misrepresentation of Him. I found this aggressiveness throughout Ezekiel with the women prophesying false information.

I will pour out my spirit upon all flesh, your sons and daughters shall prophesy. Joel 2:28

Part Five

<u>**Minor Prophets**</u>

Hosea

Joel

Amos

Obadiah

Jonah

Micah

Nahum

Habakkuk

Zephaniah

Haggai

Zechariah

Malachi

I will pour out my spirit upon all flesh, your sons and daughters shall prophesy. Joel 2:28

Chapter 10

Joel

Although Joel is classified as a minor prophet, he makes some major statements or maybe I should say he speaks a powerful prophetic word concerning the last days, as well as letting us know that God use both men and women to prophesy. Now most theologians and men of the cloth admits that these are the last days. However, they are reluctant to admit that God called women to preach, or be in any form of leadership position with authority over men. Maybe they don't know the definition of a prophet, or just maybe they are from the old school. Not only do we have our daughters as prophets, but the old men as seers, God said the young men would dream dreams and see visions. He's going to use and is using young girls and boys. Some write the women off, some write off the old and some write the young people off. Don't they know that

I will pour out my spirit upon all flesh, your sons and daughters shall prophesy. Joel 2:28

God uses whomever He pleases? He's looking for a vessel to operate through. A clean vessel, a sanctified vessel, above all, a righteous vessel. It could be a child, an elderly, male or female. God said in one portion of the scriptures, that if we don't praise Him, the trees would cry out. So let us do as the prophet Isaiah exclaimed, cry loud and spare not, let us lift up our voices like a trumpet, compelling them to come into the ark of safety. Amen.

There's no male nor female in God, nor is there any marrying, when we reach heaven. God declares that He would pour out His spirit upon ALL flesh, no respect of person, the old and young, male and female. **Joel 2:28-32.**

The book of Joel includes all genders. It clearly states the whole matter. Although prior scriptures have provided ample evidence where women have played major leadership roles from Genesis to Revelations, men yet have difficulty in digesting the fact that women can serve in such roles, and serve extremely well in them. Amen.

Food for thought. Women are important in the eyesight of God. They play an important role in the life of men, children, and our society. An old cliché the hand that rocks the cradle, rules the world.

Jeremiah was told not to marry at all. **Jeremiah 16:2.**

I will pour out my spirit upon all flesh, your sons and daughters shall prophesy. Joel 2:28

Ezekiel faced a more severe test. God took his wife that he dearly loved and commanded him not to mourn. **Ezekiel 24:16-17.**

Hosea was asked to take a wife who would be unfaithful. **Hosea 1:2 and 3:1.** God used this marriage to show Israel their spiritual adulterous life they had committed towards Him.

God let us know that He yet love us, even in our unfaithfulness through the marriage of Hosea and Gomer. God is willing to take us back in our backslidden and rebellious ways, our adulterous state of minds, ways, actions, thoughts and deeds. All we need to do is sincerely repent, be godly sorrowful for our wrongful deeds and reframe from returning back constantly into the enemies camp.

God also let us know through the experiences of Hosea, that we will not go unpunished in our disobedience.

I will pour out my spirit upon all flesh, your sons and daughters shall prophesy. Joel 2:28

PART SIX

Woman Matters

I will pour out my spirit upon all flesh, your sons and daughters shall prophesy. Joel 2:28

Chapter 11

Speaking of Woman

The Bible speaks of many women and their performances without specific names. It will just state the great woman etc.

Just a little word from the wise. I was taught, a man will always be respected as a man, it doesn't matter what he does. But a woman will be frowned upon for lowering her standards. A good Biblical example of this is in the New Testament. When they brought the woman to Jesus caught in adultery, where was the man? Be reminded, they caught her in the very act. Folks, she wasn't by herself! Where was the man? I'm sure she wasn't using adult toys! Where was the man? Jesus asked her, Where are your accusers? She answered I don't have any Lord. Jesus replied, I don't condemn you either. Discontinue living in sin, go now and live in peace, **John 8:10.** Wow, what a blow of reality that was! Women, let us remain in high standing with our

I will pour out my spirit upon all flesh, your sons and daughters shall prophesy. Joel 2:28

Lord Jesus Christ, our Savior, and keep our bodies holy and acceptable unto the Lord God. And remember the hand that rock, the cradle, rules the world. We want to be responsible for bringing up holy men like Hanna did. She dedicated the prophet Samuel to God as a young child as soon as he was weaned. I'd like to think he was about four years old when she took him to the temple to remain there with the prophet.

Genesis 25:23. Rebekah was having difficulty with her pregnancy. She directed her concern directly to the Lord God personally, as to what the struggle was going on inside of her. God explained that she was carrying two nations. One would be stronger than the other, with two different kind of people. The eldest serving the youngest. We find later in the scriptures how she schemed and helped the Lord God out in this matter. Of course it turned ugly. It always do when we decide to help God out. A separation of child and parents, a separation of siblings. Heartbreaks caused through the separation of child from his parents. All because the mother decided to help God out.

The purpose of this passage and many others, are to show that God speaks to women too. Not only did He speak to them but He used them as well. Woman are very important to God and His purpose also. Why? Because they bring

I will pour out my spirit upon all flesh, your sons and daughters shall prophesy. Joel 2:28

forth. What? Life. Jesus came down through the linage of a prostitute, a woman by the name of Rahab.

When you study the Bible, you are so enlightened. For example, Rahab wasn't just a prostitute, she was a business woman. She manufactured and dyed fabric, to be exact, fine linen fabric. Rahab was a clever woman. This is shown when she hid the men of God. Thus allowing the children of Israel to fight a victorious battle. Her spiritual insight allowed her and her family to be saved.

I will pour out my spirit upon all flesh, your sons and daughters shall prophesy. Joel 2:28

Women
In
The New Testament

I will pour out my spirit upon all flesh, your sons and daughters shall prophesy. Joel 2:28

PART SEVEN

The Books of the Four Gospels

Matthew

Mark

Luke

John

I will pour out my spirit upon all flesh, your sons and daughters shall prophesy. Joel 2:28

Chapter 12

The Four Gospels

Matthew, arranged as the first book of the four gospels, list among the genealogy of Christ several women, Rachab (Rahab), Ruth, and Bathsheba. Now it doesn't state Bathsheba's name, why? I don't know but, it just states that "David begat Solomon of her that had been the wife of Urias". And we all know who that was. You guessed. Yes Bathsheba. Although Matthew gave her, her due credits, she earned them. She played an important role as the wife of King David, and the life of King Solomon her son as well. She made sure that he became king, as King David his father had promised her. Bathsheba was there at the King's feeble and dying bedside to remind him of this for their son, Solomon. **Matthew 1:5-6.**

What did all of these women have in common? They all were the mother of giant men, which remind me of an old

I will pour out my spirit upon all flesh, your sons and daughters shall prophesy. Joel 2:28

adage, "the hand that rocks the cradle, rules the world." The first woman mentioned in Matthew was Rahab, the mother of Boaz. What a great love story that is. Boaz a wealthy and honorable man, from the tribe of Juda, married Ruth. Perhaps, being that Boaz was the product of his mother a harlot, is why he protected Ruth in her advances towards him. Boaz and Ruth was the parents of Obed. Obed was the father of Jessie, which is the father of David. This gives us a glimpse of the family tree Jesus Christ our Lord and Savior was born into. Remember He came down through forty-two generations.

I would like to provoke a little humor in this passage of scripture. The Bible states that the man that finds a wife, finds a good thing. Well Ruth pursued Boaz and found a real good thing. Not only was he good, he was wealthy too.

Later, **Matthew 1:16**, tells us that Jacob was the father of Joseph. And Joseph was the chosen husband of Mary. Mary is the chosen mother of Jesus Christ our Lord and Savior. Mary was a special vessel for the birth of our Lord Jesus Christ our Savior, brought into this world to save us from our many sins. Mary had not slept with a man, she was pure, clean, a virgin which gave birth through the Holy Ghost. God sent His angel Gabriel to let her know she was blessed and highly favored with God on her side. She would

I will pour out my spirit upon all flesh, your sons and daughters shall prophesy. Joel 2:28

be giving birth to the Son of the Highest. Mary went into a song of praise, magnifying and praising our Lord God for such a great honor that He had placed on her. Mary rejoiced in knowing that she would be regarded as blessed throughout all generations. Amen. Found in the book of **Luke 1:36-46.**

If only we had more virgins marrying today. Just maybe the divorce court wouldn't be so flooded, neither would there be so many one parent homes and children without the knowledge of whom their fathers and sometimes mothers are. The adoption agencies running over with mothers giving up their children for adoption because the child was born out of wedlock. The jail houses full of our children because of so much violence. Drugs on the rampage, all because of the big act and small three letter word called sin. Also adultery and fornication, in other words sex without being married to the person. Sin breeding more sin. One mother six children and six different fathers, or one father six children, and six different mothers.

God is looking for clean vessels, like unto virgins, untouched by the devil, or cleaned up from the devil. Say to the devil, you can't touch me. I belong to God. A clean vessel can be male or female. If you're not clean, God made it possible for us to become clean, set apart for Him through

I will pour out my spirit upon all flesh, your sons and daughters shall prophesy. Joel 2:28

His Son, Jesus Christ. It doesn't matter if you've sinned in your pass. God is willing to forgive you and throw it in the sea of forgetfulness. What a blessing!

I like the way **Doctor Luke 2:36-38**, expresses the presence of Anna the prophetess, as the daughter of Phanuel, tribe of Aser. Anna was the recipient of a prosperous tribe. The tribe of Aser was known for its prosperity and olive oil. Anna was known as the faithful to the Lord God, and for her virginity throughout the death of her seventh year of marriage. Thus leaving her a young widow for eighty-four years. The Bible doesn't state whether she had children or not, neither does it state the husband's name. But it does specify that she was married as a virgin, and continued to be a virgin after the death of her husband of seven years. She was dedicated to God with fasting and prayer day and night never leaving the temple. She was faithful through her youth all the way through her December years of at least ninety-two or more years of age. This is the part I like, Anna was there for any and all that came looking for salvation, meaning she taught and preached Jesus. I don't believe she discriminated, nor was she bothered to think of herself as being a woman, nor was she looked upon as a woman, but a prophet of God. She simply led people to God, men women, boys and girls all alike. Never stopping to

I will pour out my spirit upon all flesh, your sons and daughters shall prophesy. Joel 2:28

think I'm a woman. But preaching the unadulterated word of God, through the inspiration of God, both day and night to all that was searching for redemption. In other words, Anna was used by God to bring people to Him, in the New Testament. Anna, a female prophetess/preacher in the New Testament.

We need more Annas in our day and time. It amazes me to see some of our elderly doing the same things as the youth, smoking, drinking, drugging, murdering, stealing, and lusting after the flesh and so on. In some cases the older teaches the younger generation, the ropes. They lead by example, doing the wrong thing. Some things are so dark, they are not to be mentioned.

The New Testament mentions six Mary's'. The first one mentioned above is Mary the mother of Jesus Christ (**Luke 2:7**). The second one is Mary Magdalene (**Luke 7:37**), whom Jesus cast out seven demons. She was there at the crucifixion, and the one who tried to comfort Jesus during His suffering at the crucifixion. She was also there at His mock trial. She was the first witness of Jesus resurrection and sent to tell His disciples, to tell them He had risen. The third Mary, was the Mary of Bethany (**Luke 10:38-42),** Martha and Lazarus's sister. The Mary that sat at the feet of Jesus while he taught. The Mary that anointed

I will pour out my spirit upon all flesh, your sons and daughters shall prophesy. Joel 2:28

the feet of Jesus with that expensive oil, spikenard. Jesus gave her the honors of her acts as being a memorial. Mary number four, the mother of James and Joses (**Matthew 27:55**). Her presence were also at the tomb of Jesus to anoint His body with spices, only to discover that He was no longer numbered among the dead. Mary number five, the mother of John Mark, the great writer of the gospel of Mark. Prayer meetings were held in her home. As a results of the prayer meetings held in her home, Peter was released from prison by a divine angel. Mary number six. Although little is mentioned in her behalf, she is noted for being an outstanding Christian in Rome as one that labored much among the saints of God, greeted by Paul.

Matthew 25:1. This passage of scripture symbolizes the kingdom of heaven to ten virgin women. Heaven is clean, filled with joy, peace, righteousness and truth. The scriptures signifies that we should be ready at all times, with the Holy Ghost always on board. Because we don't know the day nor the hour the Son of man will return. Therefore it behoove us to be ready at all times. We don't have time to pick daises nor take chances on letting down our hair, thinking we have grace that will cover us before the door close or the rapture comes.

I will pour out my spirit upon all flesh, your sons and daughters shall prophesy. Joel 2:28

Matthew 27:19. Pilate's wife, a woman had more vision of Jesus and His righteousness than her husband did. She perceived that Jesus was and is the Christ, therefore she instructed her husband to have nothing to do with the death of our Savior. The Lord showed her in a dream that He wasn't just an ordinary man. Did Pilate listen to her? No, of course not. He listen to the multitude, which were probably made up of mostly men crying, crucify Him! Sorry men. But usually women are more compassionate.

I will pour out my spirit upon all flesh, your sons and daughters shall prophesy. Joel 2:28

PART EIGHT

The Book of History

Acts

I will pour out my spirit upon all flesh, your sons and daughters shall prophesy. Joel 2:28

Chapter 13

Women through the Eyes of Apostle Paul

The book of Acts, divinely written by Paul, inspired by our Lord and Savior Jesus Christ, gives an abundance of credit to women in authority.

Acts 8:3. Paul persecuted both men and women alike, throwing them in prison, thus treating them equally. Which meant they all were believers, participating in the worship of Christ.

We also find in **Acts 8:12**, that both men and women were baptized. I don't know of what importance it was to voice, but **verse 27,** mentions that an eunuch (a man) with great authority was under the great leadership of queen Candace (a woman) of Ethiopia, in charge of the treasure (all the money). This indicates that she was a woman of high standing, trustworthy, and a woman of great power and authority. She

I will pour out my spirit upon all flesh, your sons and daughters shall prophesy. Joel 2:28

journeyed from Ethiopia as well as to Jerusalem with the intentions of worshipping God.

In **Acts 9:1-3**, we find that Paul sought after both men and women disciples to persecute and slaughter if they professed Jesus Christ as their Lord and Savior. I feel that if the women weren't a threat to the male dominated pulpit, preaching the Word of God, and just passive listeners, Paul would not have abducted them with the men believers. But since they too were expounders, thus bringing unbelievers into the fold, they were also persecuted same as the men.

Acts 9:35, There was a prosperous business women named Lydia. She was the first convert to Christianity in Macedonia and in all of Europe as a disciple of Christ.

Later in **Acts, chapter 16:12-16**, Lydia is mentioned again. As a fact during their stay in Macedonia (Paul, Peter and the disciples) had a meeting with the women there. It was during this union that God opened Lydia's heart, she was baptized, and there she accepted Christ Jesus as her personal savior as well as her entire household.

As far as I can see and tell, when Jesus made converts, He summonsed them to go in peace and sin no more. But, they immediately began spreading the word, telling all they came into contact with, the good news and preaching the gospel, both men and women. Although He would often

I will pour out my spirit upon all flesh, your sons and daughters shall prophesy. Joel 2:28

say tell no one, they would blast it. They couldn't keep it to themselves. Now Peter said it this way, "God is no respect of person, **Acts 10:34**". My mom would say it this way, God use whomever He want, wherever He want, when He want. Furthermore, who's to say that these women weren't leaders? According to my understanding of the Bible, Lydia was holding service in her home, and Paul was preaching. She was already a worshipper of God, but after hearing Paul's preaching, she became a devout Christian.

Also in the same chapter verse 36, Tabitha also known as Dorcas, was a Business woman that manufactured clothes, and a giver of money to the poor. She was a woman that did much good during her time. But when she died, many grieved her death. She was so well loved until their faith and Peter's prayers brought her back from death to life. That's what I call genuine love. I don't recall any of the men being loved this much. I'm sorry yes there was Lazarus.

Acts 12:12-18. I believe it was the women that initiated and held the intercessory prayer, which caused Peter to be released and led from jail. No doubt it was both men and women there in her home, however, Mary was the one in charge. Why? Because the Bible states that the service was held at her house, the mother of John Mark. And a

I will pour out my spirit upon all flesh, your sons and daughters shall prophesy. Joel 2:28

young lady named Rhoda answered the door when Peter knocked, thus indicating clearly that the prayer meeting was held with a group of dedicated women. Another give-a-way is that Peter makes a statement, commissioning them (the women), to go and tell James, and the brethren (the men) how the Lord God had delivered him out of prison, due to the intercessory prayer held by the women of God. Woman can also get a prayer through! They know how to touch the heart of God. Amen. One portion of scripture reads like this, call for the praying and cunning women.

Acts 13:50, the tide has turned, now Paul is being persecuted. The Jews stirred up the people, both men and women of great integrity against the teachings of Paul and Barnabas and ran them out of their township. Paul also mentions honorable women in this chapter. I researched the word honorable. I like the one which said a title of distinction.

Acts 16:13-15, Apostle Paul introduce us to Lydia which lived in Thyatira as an outstanding and prosperous business woman of God. Lydia used her money to further the gospel of Jesus Christ. She was a worshiper of God, became a <u>devout</u> Christian and was baptized after hearing the teachings of Paul.

I will pour out my spirit upon all flesh, your sons and daughters shall prophesy. Joel 2:28

Acts 17:4, 12 and 34. The Apostle Paul gives more credence to women than any other single writer in the Bible according to my recollection. He didn't just mention women, he was very descriptive with adjectives, although some of the women were nameless. They were identified by their rank, title and or status. For example, he mentions <u>chief</u> women, again the word <u>chief</u> is worth defining. We often use the phrase, "everybody want to be a Chief and no Indians", meaning everyone wants to lead and no followers. To me chief means the leader or the authority, to rule over a group of people. Webster Dictionary defines it as: 1. "One who is highest in rank or authority; leader, 2. A boss. 3. The highest or most important part of something. 4. Highest in rank authority or office.

Therefore the significance of calling this no name woman a chief leads me to believe that she was an important leader. Not only were there women in leadership, but according to Paul they were in large numbers, not a few he says.

Later in the same chapter, verse 12, he mentions <u>honorable</u> women. To me an <u>honorable</u> woman is one that's looked up to and well respected. However, we will visit Webster again. These are some of the meanings it provided: 1. Deserving or winning honor and respect. 2. Bringing

I will pour out my spirit upon all flesh, your sons and daughters shall prophesy. Joel 2:28

distinction or recognition. 3. Consistent with honor or a good name.

So as we can see, these were not common, ordinary women. They were devout women of God. They were leaders of Tribes and communities. I believe they had political power as well as the men did.

Acts 21:9, Apostle Paul let us know that during their voyage to Macedonia, they came into contact with an Evangelist named Phillip. Why he felt the need to mention Phillip with four preaching daughters, I don't know. Maybe because Evangelist Phillip was a disciple of Jesus Christ or just maybe it was of importance to include it in the scriptures to let us know that female preachers are approved by God in the New Testament as well as the Old Testament. We all do agree, that the prophets were people divinely inspired by God, thus He spoke to them. God spoke to Eve, and Sarah in the Old Testament. God spoke to Mary the mother of Jesus in the New Testament. Yes, God spoke to women in both the Old and New Testaments consisting of virgins and prophetess. God had women prophets in both the Old and New Testaments. Again, what are prophets? The answer, preachers. I'm sure Evangelist Phillip's family had a Holy Ghost good time in the Lord with all of those

I will pour out my spirit upon all flesh, your sons and daughters shall prophesy. Joel 2:28

preachers in one household. Can you imagine four preaching women along with their father a preacher as well under one roof? Amen.

After reading the passage showing Philip's daughters as preachers. I was reminded of Paul, when he was on the other side of the fence, persecuting both men and women. Because they both were a threat to him. Therefore, he imprisoned and murdered both men and women.

I will pour out my spirit upon all flesh, your sons and daughters shall prophesy. Joel 2:28

Part Nine

The Pauline Epistles

Romans
I Corinthians
II Corinthians
Galatians
Ephesians
Philippians
Colossians
I Thessalonians
II Thessalonians
I Timothy
II Timothy
Titus
Philemon
Hebrew

I will pour out my spirit upon all flesh, your sons and daughters shall prophesy. Joel 2:28

Chapter 14

Women in Ministry

Paul declares in **Romans 2:11**, that there is no respect of person with God. All have sinned and came short of the glory of God, therefore all must repent and be baptized in Jesus, or otherwise we perish.

Romans 16:1-2. *I commend unto you Phebe our sister, which is a servant of the church which is at Cenchrea: That you receive her in the Lord, as being a saint, and that you assist her in whatsoever business she has need of you: for she has been a succorer of many, and of myself also. Greet Priscilla and Aquila my helpers in Christ Jesus: Who have for my life laid down their own necks; unto whom not only I give thanks, but also all the churches of the Gentiles.*

I will pour out my spirit upon all flesh, your sons and daughters shall prophesy. Joel 2:28

What is a saint and what is a succorer? Why do you suppose Paul wanted these women to be received?

Webster gave several definitions of being a <u>saint.</u> One, a person officially recognized by canonization as being entitled to public veneration and capable of interceding for people on earth, and two a member of any of various religious groups. Next, the word <u>succorer,</u> which means assist or help in time of distress according to Webster Dictionary.

I supposed Paul insist that these women be recognized as such because they were holding the women back just as they are doing today in some churches and organizations.

Galatians 3:8. According to Apostle Paul, "there is neither Jew nor Greek, bond nor free, male nor female, for we are all one in Christ Jesus".

In God, there is no respect of person. He spoke through both male and female, in the Old and the New Testaments. He uses whom He will whenever He want too. All He need is a willing and sincere heart.

In **Philippians 4:3**, Paul made a statement while speaking to Euodias a Christian woman, and Syntyche another female Christian which lead me to believe that these women were at odds with each other in their mission for the Lord. He admonished the two of them to be in

I will pour out my spirit upon all flesh, your sons and daughters shall prophesy. Joel 2:28

agreement having the same mind. He also instructed his co-labors to help those women which labored with him and Clement, his co-laborer in the gospel. What do you suppose these women were doing? What is laboring in the gospel? They were teaching and preaching, bringing new converts to Christ Jesus. God don't care who preach and teach His Word. It could be a child, woman, or a man. This is evident throughout the Bible, both Old and New Testaments. Mary carried the Word for nine months inside of her, Baby Jesus. After nine months of carrying the Word, then she gave birth to the Word.

I Timothy 2:9-15, we see Paul spending teachable moments with his spiritual son Timothy. We should have the Word of God in us likewise, so much that it will allow us to do the same such teachings as Paul did with our youth of today.

Paul taught Timothy good morals, how to be spiritual, humble, and have intercessory pray, not just for himself, but for all mankind both small and great. He taught him how to live in a peaceable manner towards all. Not only did he give these instructions to Timothy, but he then turned and addressed it to the women as well. Letting them know that they too had to exemplify Christ in all of their manners and dress wear. He taught them to be innocent and not brazing,

I will pour out my spirit upon all flesh, your sons and daughters shall prophesy. Joel 2:28

in other words women, have some respect for yourselves. Keep yourselves pleasing to God in all and everything you wear and do.

This portion of the scriptures is where men hold fast to. **Verse 12,** women should not usurp authority over men. I suffer a woman not to teach. Notice he said "I". Well, what do we do with the portion of scripture where Paul also said Timothy was taught well by his Jew/Christian mother and grandmother? I don't know where Timothy's biological father was, who was a Roman, maybe a Roman Catholic but the scriptures plainly let us know who taught him. Also Paul admonished his fellow workers to go down and help those women that labor in the gospel. I see two things Paul is saying in this portion of scripture. One he uses the word "I", meaning this is something he himself is saying. Paul interjected a lot of things the way he himself saw it, or as it applied to the occasion, place or situation he was involved in at that particular time. He didn't say it was coming from God. Two, he was talking to a certain group of people. The women probably had a takeover spirit, you know, like some people of today have. They want to do everything themselves. Always criticizing everyone and everything that's done by someone else.

I will pour out my spirit upon all flesh, your sons and daughters shall prophesy. Joel 2:28

According to Webster's Dictionary, the word <u>usurp</u> means; 1. To seize and hold, such as the power, position or rights of another by force and without legal right or authority. 2. To take over or occupy physically such as territory or possessions. To seize another's power.

Women don't try to be a man, we're not men. Although we're equal in Christ Jesus, we're different in gender and the role we play. I love being a woman. If you know how or if not learn how. Through this you can be a great ruler, one with great authority through the auspice of your husband. You know, like plant the idea in his mind and let him believe it was his. The first lady Abigale Adams of the United States did. She constantly reminded her husband John Adams, the second President of the United States, "Don't forget the woman". She opposed to the fact that married women couldn't own property nor have say in the political arena. Maybe she read the portion of scripture where the five daughters of Zalophehad didn't have sons, so his five daughters demanded that they be given portions of the property as well as those who had sons. **Numbers 27:1-5**. Abigale was an advisor to her husband. This goes back to the old saying, "behind every great man is a great woman". Although I don't know how much validity or accuracy it has but, it has been said many times that Hillary Clinton

I will pour out my spirit upon all flesh, your sons and daughters shall prophesy. Joel 2:28

was the one ruling the United States, behind the auspice of her husband Bill Clinton. However, when she stepped up to the plate to consider running for President, to me certainly proved the saying to be true whether or not it is.

I love my positions as a woman of God, daughter, sister, wife and, mother, last but not least, Pastor and Overseer. It gives me the opportunity to help people in a greater way. If you are more knowledgeable than your spouse, please don't degrade them, help them if you can, to come up to par as much as their ability will allow them, if they will let you. If your spouse is called to be a leader, don't be a hindrance, be a helpmate. This does not apply to spiritual only but also in the corporate world. Whatever your spouse endeavor to do help them.

1 Peter 3:1-7. Peter mentions the mannerism of women, their poise and character. He also expounds on what the care for them should be steaming from the men. Peter expresses love and kindness towards them. He believed that an unbelieving spouse can be won over to Christ by the believing spouse. Now when we are under the subjection of a spouse, it work two ways. One, we are under their authority and two, they are responsible for our wellbeing. Now here's the twist, we are under subjection to each other. Never is it one sided. In exemplifying this, Peter used the word

I will pour out my spirit upon all flesh, your sons and daughters shall prophesy. Joel 2:28

"likewise" frequently, speaking to both husband and wife. Paul wasn't one sided, he advocated the same treatment for both sides husband and wife alike. Two more things worth mentioning is that we should be beautiful both on the inside as well as the outside. Because the outside adorning really doesn't count in the eye sight of God, it is what's in the heart.

I will continue to say and advocate that women as mothers are the first teachers, trainers, and molders of men's lives during their infancy through manhood. Very sad to say, but many fathers of today are nowhere to be found or refuse to take responsibility of the upbringing of their children, especially the males. Yet it only gives the mother the role to be a mother not both mother and father. We cannot take the place of a man, nor can a man take the place of a woman. I thank God for my sons and their father, he was and they are there for their children.

II Timothy 1:5. Women bring forth and produce. Timothy is a product of two women's teaching. His mother Eunice and grandmother Lois. Paul reminds him not to forget those teaching and his upbringing. It is undeniable clear that Paul gives this credit of Timothy's Christian teaching of the scriptures to those two women.

I will pour out my spirit upon all flesh, your sons and daughters shall prophesy. Joel 2:28

Since Paul gives more credit to positive things of women, I am even more led to believe that when he himself asked women not to speak and be quiet, that this was an isolated situation, for a special reason.

II Timothy 4:19/Romans 16:3 – Acts 18:2, 1, 8 and **verse 26**. Here in **Second Timothy,** Paul greets a husband and wife team, Priscilla and Aquila. Priscilla and Aquila are made mentioned several times in the scriptures, which seem to be of some great degree of importance. Not only that but I noticed that Pricilla's name is mentioned first and more frequent than her husband. However, they as leaders headed a church in their home together as a husband and wife team. As I view it, this was a dedicated couple working close together side by side with one accord in the Gospel of faith in our Lord and Savior Jesus Christ. **I Corinthians 16:19**

Titus 2:3. Here Paul is giving good sound doctrine and teaching to both men and women. He is instructing that living a righteous life is for all young and old. It doesn't matter what age nor gender. We must be sober minded, love each other, be clean, obedient, teachers of righteousness, have patience, and be a good examples for others to see and desire to live this Christian walk daily.

One Bible scholar J. Rendel Harris, believed that the book of **Hebrews** may have been written by Priscila a

I will pour out my spirit upon all flesh, your sons and daughters shall prophesy. Joel 2:28

woman Aquila's wife. While others yet have different viewpoints as to whom the author is. The most important fact is that it is the Word of God and full of goodies to help us on this Christian journey.

Hebrews 11:11/Genesis 17:19 – 18:11, 14 and 21:2. The woman Sarah is mentioned in the Hall of Faith along with the other believers of God, although she is at the age of 90, she will be the one to carry the fruitful seed of her husband Abraham 100 years old, and give birth to a son, thus fulfilling the promise/covenant from God.

Hebrews 11:23, does not state that the Faith was through three women, Moses mother, sister, and Pharaoh's daughter, that saved his life as a three month old infant. Instead it states that he was hidden by his parents after seeing that he was a special male child. I'm going to go with the Old Testament that he was hid through his mother and sister and rescued by Pharaoh's daughter. Nowhere does it mention his father in this particular transaction. Not to say that the father didn't have a say, he was there according to **Acts.** But, the scriptures we have to go by put inferences on the mother and sister in **Exodus. Exodus 1:16** and **verse 20 – Exodus 2:2** and **Acts 7:20.**

Hebrews 11:31/Joshua 2:1 - 6:23 – James 2:25. By faith, the harlot Rahab, a woman, saved her entire family

I will pour out my spirit upon all flesh, your sons and daughters shall prophesy. Joel 2:28

from perishing. She believed that if she helped to protect the people of God, she and her family would be saved and not destroyed with the unbelievers.

Out of the eleven verses pertaining to <u>faith</u> in the **eleventh chapter** of **Hebrews,** only two mention women. Actually four should have, but the other two, their rights were taken. One, **verse 23**, mentions Moses parents when in fact it was his mother. If you read **Exodus 2:2,** it plainly tell you that Moses's mother gave birth to him and saw he was a blessed child, saved him at three months old. As far as I can see, even the mid-wives (women) had a part in this too, they disobeyed Pharos orders to kill all boy babies born to the Hebrew women. The unknown author mentions the father of Moses in a roundabout way in **Acts 7:20,** that is to say that Moses was three months old in his fathers' house. It is evident that a man was around, otherwise there would be no conception of children. **Verse 32** verifies Barak as a hero and others, not including the women, Deborah and Jael. If we go to **Judges 4:1-24** and **Judges 5:1-31**, there we will find that the faith was through Judge Deborah rather than Barak. My point of view is, Barak exemplified more faith in Judge Deborah than he did God. Why do I say this? Because he refused to go into battle without her. Barak was listed as a hero in **Hebrew Chapter eleven verse 32**. But

I will pour out my spirit upon all flesh, your sons and daughters shall prophesy. Joel 2:28

as far as I am concerned, here again, according to the Old Testament scriptures, the victory was given to a woman, Jael a shero as Judge Deborah had prophesied. Barak was full of fear, plus he worried about the size and the amount of iron chariots King Jabin and his captain Sisera's army consist of. Judge Deborah summonsed Barak, gave him what thus said the Lord God Almighty had given her. That was to take ten thousand soldiers, go out and you will be victorious, but through a woman.

Well it seems that the unknown author of Hebrews fell down on the job here. Because the credit of Jail and Moses mom was given to men. Why? I don't know. However, I do know that the women were not given any credit whatsoever for these two huge accomplishments in the New Testament. On those premises I don't think Priscilla was the author of Hebrews. Because she being a woman herself, I believe wouldn't have left these two important factors out of the women's history.

It pays to search the scriptures and study the Word of God for yourself. Amen.

I'm truly convinced that women did so much more in the Bible days. But was never given credit for it, just like **Hebrews 11:32**. I remember my children's father admitting to me one day that one of his friends came over and admired

I will pour out my spirit upon all flesh, your sons and daughters shall prophesy. Joel 2:28

the décor of our home. He admitted that he told him he himself did it. His statement to me was, "I'm sorry Shirley, and I must admit that I took all of your credit away from you today."

I will pour out my spirit upon all flesh, your sons and daughters shall prophesy. Joel 2:28

PART TEN

General Epistles

James

I Peter

II Peter

I John

II John

III John

Jude

I will pour out my spirit upon all flesh, your sons and daughters shall prophesy. Joel 2:28

Chapter 15

Exhortations for Women in the General Epistles

Although Rahab was labeled as a Harlot, she made great contributions in the Old Testament. They were revealed in both the Old and New Testaments. Rahab was also a business woman, she manufactured dyed linen. Rahab was an ancestor of David and Jesus Christ, they came down through her linage. She was the mother of Boaz. Boaz was the husband of Ruth with that great historic and romantic love story.

Rahab was a shero in the Hall of Faith **Hebrew 11:31.** You will find her in four different books of the Bible, one in the Old Testament, twice in the book of Joshua, and three books in the New Testament:

Joshua 2:1-21

Joshua 6:17-25

I will pour out my spirit upon all flesh, your sons and daughters shall prophesy. Joel 2:28

Matthew 1:5

Hebrew 11:31

James 2:25

Brother James extended another link to Rahab as being justified for her works. Her work was exemplified through her faith when she hid the messengers, believing for the safety for her family.

Sarah

First Peter 3:5-6. I thank God Peter does not put this honor as one sided. It is shown when he use the word "likewise". I found these exhortations given many times in the New Testament. It wasn't just given to the women to obey, love and respect their husbands but for the men to do likewise to their wives. Work with them according to their knowledge. Some women are extremely enlightened in the secular world as well as in the Word of God. You can't treat a woman with knowledge, and or wisdom like one that's short coming in these areas of understanding.

I will pour out my spirit upon all flesh, your sons and daughters shall prophesy. Joel 2:28

Women weren't made to be treated like second class citizens, neither should they be treated as such. I've seen in some organizations, the men sit in the pulpit while the women sit below them, as to say you are not worthy. The women are classified as missionaries and evangelist whereas Paul was the first missionary (a man). I do see men in the Caucasian churches as missionaries but little and rarely do I see it in the Afro American Pentecostal churches.

Sarah is shown here in the New Testament as a woman that put her husband up high. She looked up to him as lord. One part of the scripture tell us that Abraham loved Sarah too.

****

I would like to bring into focus a few couples working together as a team and rewarded for their good and or bad behavior as a team, in the Old and New Testaments.

First we have Adam and Eve in the **Old Testament**. Eve conspired to sin and lured her husband into it as well. Now they both were guilty of sinning against God. However, Adam was given the instructions of what to and what not to eat. They were one in their disobedience to God's command. Husband and wife therefore both suffered. Because of their

I will pour out my spirit upon all flesh, your sons and daughters shall prophesy. Joel 2:28

sin, Adam now had to work by the sweat of his brow and Eve would have pain in her child bearing.

Later we have Queen Jezebel and King Ahab working together, sinned through serving as worshippers of Baal. Jezebel committed murder for her husband, but Ahab was also accused of it as well, **I Kings 21:19**. She took another man's property and gave it to her husband, King Ahab. As a result, she was rewarded for the wickedness she committed, a horrible death. A death where she was beyond recognition, with nothing to bury her by but memories. Although King Ahab did great evil in the sight of God as well, he did have sense enough to repent. He went on a fast and was godly sorrowful for his sins. God declared that because of his humility, evil would not come during the day of his Kingship, instead it would fall in the day of his offspring's. Therefore, it behoove us to do the right thing before our God. Because we don't want our sins to fall on our children, thus causing them to reap punishment for sins we committed. I remember praying many times during my child rearing, "Lord please don't let my sins fall on my children." **I Kings 16:29-31**

Next we have Ananias and Sapphira, in the **New Testament**. They too purposed in their heart to commit sin by lying to the man of God. They both had their story

I will pour out my spirit upon all flesh, your sons and daughters shall prophesy. Joel 2:28

together of what they would say. Now it was their own property to do as they wish. However, they chose to sell it for a price and lie about the amount it was sold for. They both were dishonest and lied. They both died at the foot of the Prophet. **Acts 5:1-10.** This type of action can be identified with some people of today, in paying their tithes. They pay it to be much less than what it actually is, not knowing they are causing damage to come upon them. This is called dishonesty. Know this, we must give an account of all things done and said in our bodies.

Then we have another couple in the **New Testament,** Aquilla and Priscilla. They worked as a team, being true children of God. **Acts 18:2. Acts 18:26,** Aquila and Priscilla both took Apollos of Alexandria under their wings and taught him the correct way of God's baptism. They were his mentors in the Word of the Lord. Apollos only knew the way of John's baptism, now he knew it God's way. Not only that but now he was ready to be accepted by the disciples of Christ and expound the Word of God more profoundly, using the scriptures to teach the Jews that Jesus is the Christ.

I will pour out my spirit upon all flesh, your sons and daughters shall prophesy. Joel 2:28

PART ELEVEN

Book of Prophecy

Revelations

I will pour out my spirit upon all flesh, your sons and daughters shall prophesy. Joel 2:28

Chapter 16

Prophecy

Revelations 17:3-7. I believe that this portion of the Bible scriptures deal with our country, the United States of America. That is, it's being fashioned as an adulterous woman. The prophetic word is letting us know what the end of times are going to be like, here in the United States of America. Because of its state of fornication and many corruptible acts that's being committed.

God has really blessed The United States of America. But the United States of America have once again turned their backs on God and doing every corruptible thing they can think of. We now call what was once wrong, right, and what was right, now it's wrong. We don't have the freedom to pray in our schools nor public domain anymore. We must be careful how we discipline our offspring's. Once certain things were kept in the closet, now it's out and considered

I will pour out my spirit upon all flesh, your sons and daughters shall prophesy. Joel 2:28

correct. No shame or stigmas are attached. Equality for all the things we considered as constitutional and Biblical wrong before and during my life time, is now constitutional correct.

We have been warned through disasters such as 911. We were brought back into the reality of honoring God for a little while. Momentarily we found the churches full of folks, we spoke and was courteous towards each other. Soon afterwards, we went back into our old selves again. That is mean, full of hate, committing evil acts such as lying, stealing, cheating and having a nasty mean disposition towards each other. Don't believe it? Observe commuters on the subways pushing and shelving, or our motorist. And you will soon see drivers refusing to allow another motorist to move over, and if they do manage to get over, they my might get cursed out by the road-rager, or cut off, sometimes causing a severe accident.

Again, we have become more blatant with same sex relationships and marriages. Once upon a time it was hidden or may I say kept in the closet. Now a days children are coming to school saying they have two mommies. Which is a confusing situation to me. How can we fit sex education into that? The real kicker is that we offend people when we mention our Lord and Savior Jesus Christ. But it's ok to use

I will pour out my spirit upon all flesh, your sons and daughters shall prophesy. Joel 2:28

all kind of profanity. You can lose your job if you are caught practicing or discussing any religious performance. But it's ok to have music that plays with profanity in it. We are a mixed up and confused generation.

Yes America, our country is fashioned after a woman, and you America is going to perish, be destroyed. Why? Because she forgot about her first love, God Himself, and turned to the accuser that old devil and his angles.

I will pour out my spirit upon all flesh, your sons and daughters shall prophesy. Joel 2:28

PART TWELVE

Women from the Eighteen Century to the Twenty-First Century

I will pour out my spirit upon all flesh, your sons and daughters shall prophesy. Joel 2:28

Chapter 17

Women Achievers

This last chapter of the book will deal with some of our notable women from the Eighteenth to the Twenty-First Century, their accomplishments, inventions and strengths will be illuminated. Just a few will be mentioned exposing their category, be it sports, politics, education, or business, they are all of excellence.

Name	Achievements
Madam C. Walker	America's first Black female self-made millionaire.
Abigale Adams	Rights for women to vote and the expansion for women in the public eye.
Hedy Lamarr	Wireless Communication Inventor.

I will pour out my spirit upon all flesh, your sons and daughters shall prophesy. Joel 2:28

Sybilla Masters	Inventor of turning corn into cornmeal. But in husband's name Thomas.
Mary Kies	First American woman to earn a Patient in her name in 1809. She developed a way of weaving straw into hats.
Elizabeth Colman	First Black female Pilot.
Mary Anderson	Invented windshield whippers.
Mary McLeod Bethune	Noted for the genesis of a school for young African American girls and an activist as a presidential adviser for many of our country's leaders.
Grace Hooper	invented the first computer language.
Sojourner Truth	A Preacher of God's Word. Famous for her 1851 speech "Aint I A Woman."
Marion Donavan	Inventor of disposable diapers.
Shirley Chisholm	First Black woman to be elected to Congress.

I will pour out my spirit upon all flesh, your sons and daughters shall prophesy. Joel 2:28

In the above list of women in this chapter are leaders, inventors, politicians, preachers, educators, a pilot, business women, and oratories.

From Genesis to Revelation, from past to present, women have played an important and powerful role in shaping the society and will continue to do so as long as the earth exist and male babies are born. However, credit wasn't given then, as well as now. During the 19th Century women weren't able to own property. Whereas we see not only were they allowed to own property in the Bible days, but they also ruled over their tribe. By these actions, we are missing out on vast progress in both our secular and religious worlds. Leadership isn't control, but ruling with dignity and poise and not an iron fist.

I will pour out my spirit upon all flesh, your sons and daughters shall prophesy. Joel 2:28

Conclusion

Within my studies and research, these are my findings along with my own personal conclusions. Among them you will also find many Bible references.

There are three large debates in the secular and church society worldwide. One, is Jesus and God the same person or are there three Gods? Two, the role of women in the church, can they be ordained as preachers and pastors? And three, how women should dress. You will find the answer to whether or not Jesus and God the same person in my book "Is Jesus God". Next the role of women in the church, is in this book titled "Women Preachers Forbidden or not". And the dress code for women is in the makings also. So look for it in the near future.

Woman have been in leadership since the Bible days up until to date. Although it may have been undercover, like Abigale Adams was in the nineteenth century. She was responsible for the rights of women to vote and more exposure

I will pour out my spirit upon all flesh, your sons and daughters shall prophesy. Joel 2:28

in the public eye. She wrote letters and worked through her husband's presidency. Also a woman by the name of Sybilla Masters' the inventor of turning corn into cornmeal but had to patent it in her husband's name, because it was considered as property and women couldn't own property.

I can yet hear the voice of my former pastor, his famous saying was, "If I walked in a church with no women, and it had men only, my first and last sermon would be brethren fare ye well".

I maintain in my conclusion that woman are, have been, and always will be a part of the leadership role. Not trying to take the place nor rule a man, but merely using her God given skills as the Bible states through Apostle Paul. Use them according to their knowledge, whether it be a cook, housekeeper, inventor, teacher, preacher or the president of the United States of America, she is to be honored, respected and looked up to for her abilities and capabilities, not as a downcast because of her gender.

I close with this note. Women rule and rule well, or be a follower and follow well. Be a good team player. Be feminine. Be the best in whatever God has called you to do. Follow your calling regardless to what it is, be it small or large, do it and do it well!!

Amen and Amen

I will pour out my spirit upon all flesh, your sons and daughters shall prophesy. Joel 2:28

2. https://answers.yahoo.com/questions/index?qid

3. Rediscoverint the Prothetic Role of Women enrichmentjournal.ag.org/200102/080_prothetic_role.cfm

4. //rachelheldevans.com/blog/daughters-willprophesy

5. //www.worldslastchance.com/ecourses/lessons/the-spirit.of-prophecy-ecourse/12/women-phrophets-in...

6. //biblehub.com/joshua/6-25.htm

7. //biblehub.com/joshua/2-17.htm

8. www.ernestangley.org/bible/ruth/2

9. www.women-inventors.com/

10. //www.ask.com/questions/
what-was-abigail-adams-major-accomplishments

11. //www.sciencedaily.com/
releases/2012/05/120508142662.htm

12. //science.howstuffworks.com/innovation/
innovations/10-things-that-women-invented.htm

13. //www.jewfaq.org/prophet.htm

14. 30 Black Female Leaders You Should Know About by: HelloBeautifulStaff

15. God's Word to Women: Women Prophets by:Reverand Kathryn J. Riss

16. http:stronginfaith.org/article.php?page-90

17. //www.biblegateway.com/resources/911-women-bible/ruth

I will pour out my spirit upon all flesh, your sons and daughters shall prophesy. Joel 2:28

Printed in the United States
By Bookmasters